T0247971

FOREIGN POLICY CAREERS FOR PHDS

Other Titles of Interest from Georgetown University Press

Career Diplomacy: Life and Work in the US Foreign Service, Fourth Edition
by Harry W. Kopp and John K. Naland

Careers in International Affairs, Ninth Edition
Laura E. Cressey, Barrett J. Helmer, and Jennifer E. Steffensen, editors

The PhD Parenthood Trap: Caught between Work and Family in Academia
by Kerry F. Crawford and Leah C. Windsor

Working World: Careers in International Education, Exchange, and Development, Second Edition
by Sherry Lee Mueller and Mark Overmann

FOREIGN POLICY CAREERS FOR PHDS

A PRACTICAL GUIDE TO A WORLD OF POSSIBILITIES

James Goldgeier and
Tamara Cofman Wittes

Georgetown University Press / Washington, DC

Library of Congress Cataloging-in-Publication Data

Names: Goldgeier, James M., author. | Wittes, Tamara Cofman, 1969– author.
Title: Foreign policy careers for PhDs : a practical guide to a world of possibilities / James Goldgeier and Tamara Cofman Wittes.
Description: Washington : Georgetown University Press, 2023. | Includes bibliographical references and index.
Identifiers: LCCN 2023001267 (print) | LCCN 2023001268 (ebook) | ISBN 9781647123833 (paperback) | ISBN 9781647123840 (ebook)
Subjects: LCSH: International relations—Vocational guidance. | Doctoral students—Vocational guidance. | Career development.
Classification: LCC JZ1237 .G65 2023 (print) | LCC JZ1237 (ebook) | DDC 327.023—dc23/eng/20230130
LC record available at https://lccn.loc.gov/2023001267
LC ebook record available at https://lccn.loc.gov/2023001268

∞ This paper meets the requirements of ANSI/NISO Z39.48-1992 (Permanence of Paper).

24 23   9 8 7 6 5 4 3 2 First printing

Printed in the United States of America

Cover design by Jeremy John Parker
Interior design by Paul Hotvedt

Contents

Acknowledgments   vii

Introduction: Why This Book Is for You   1

1   Working *in* Foreign Policy versus Working *on* Foreign Policy   12

2   Creating Opportunities in Graduate School   24

3   Envisioning Yourself in Policy Work   50

4   The Foreign Policy Ecosystem   62

5   Looking for a Job in Foreign Policy   83

6   Career Pathways in Foreign Policy   101

7   Making a Difference Working in Foreign Policy   121

Appendixes

A: Selected Workshops, Summer Programs, and Fellowships   133

B: Selected Washington-Area Institutions Conducting Policy-Relevant Research   137

C: Selected Networking Opportunities   140

Index   143

About the Authors   147

Acknowledgments

This project would not be what it is without the contributions of dozens of colleagues from academia, NGOs, government, and well beyond who encouraged us to pursue the project, lent us their ears and eyes along the way, and shared their questions and experiences to help inform our work.

Our greatest debt goes to those who generously shared their honest experiences and reflections about their careers with us and who allowed us to share those reflections with our readers: Mary Barton, Paul J. Bonicelli, Reuben Brigety, Susanna Campbell, Ivo Daalder, Zoe Danon, Stephen Del Rosso, Erik Durbin, Alexandra Evans, Alice Hunt Friend, Steve Galpern, Matthew Jacobs, Robert Kahn, Morgan Kaplan, Kristin Lord, Tanvi Madan, Jennifer McArdle, Paul McLachlan, Sara Plana, Barry Posen, Dafna Rand, Wesley Reisser, Mara Revkin, Susan Rice, Carla Anne Robbins, Jon Rosenwasser, William Ruger, Kori Schake, Erin Simpson, James Graham Wilson, and Rebecca Wolfe.

We are grateful to American University's School of International Service for supporting our research assistants. Zied Bouchlaghem transcribed interviews, researched fellowships and workshops, and provided other invaluable assistance, including giving us a close read of the entire manuscript. Mauricio Bello helped us finalize the manuscript.

James Hamilton and Elizabeth Saunders read the manuscript in its entirety and gave us invaluable suggestions. We are grateful to an anonymous peer reviewer for Georgetown University Press who commented on the book proposal, which provided us with helpful guidance as we launched the process. Two of the Press's reviewers for the entire manuscript, Sue Peterson and Andrew Radin, gave permission to reveal their names after completing their reviews, and we are grateful for the opportunity to publicly thank them for their comments that considerably strengthened the book.

The Bridging the Gap leadership team provided intellectual support, and the Stanford University Center for International Security and Cooperation—which is part of the Freeman Spogli Institute for International Studies, led by Michael McFaul—hosted one of the authors as a visiting scholar during the completion of this project. We are grateful for all we have learned over the years from our colleagues at the Brookings Institution.

Aysha Chowdhry shared her list of Washington think tanks. Jennifer Brinkerhoff shared the book she wrote with Derick Brinkerhoff, *Working for Change: Making a Career in International Public Service*, as well as other materials that proved extremely helpful to our thinking. A Bridging the Gap webinar on nonacademic careers for PhDs held in October 2020—which included panelists Alexandra Evans, Bonnie Jenkins, Kristin Lord, Jung Pak, Erin Simpson, and Rebecca Wolfe—provided much helpful guidance.[1]

Many colleagues shared comments, ideas, advice, and experiences with us that helped shape the manuscript, including Deborah Avant, Agneska Bloch, Mietek Boduszyński, Daniel Drezner, Lee Feinstein, Ibrahim Fraihat, Vedrana Hadzialic, Rebecca Hamm, Alexander Lennon, Alicia Phillips Mandaville, Yehudah Mirsky, John Mongan, Suzanne Nossel, Elizabeth Nugent, Afshon Ostovar, Alexandra Samuel, Theodore Schuur, Mark Shulman, Joshua Sinai, Amanda Sloat, Mira Sucharov, Eric Trager, Kent Walker, and Diana Walsh.

We thank Don Jacobs, our wonderful editor at Georgetown University Press, for his immediate enthusiasm for the project, his editorial insights, and for shepherding us through the process. We are also grateful to Alfred Imhoff, Elizabeth Sheridan, Leila Sebastian, and Virginia Veiga Bryant for their assistance with, respectively, copyediting, production, and marketing at Georgetown University Press.

Finally, we are fortunate to have drawn inspiration and support from our families, who always believe in us.

Note

1. Bridging the Gap, "Virtual Panel on Non-academic Careers," October 15, 2020, https://youtu.be/pRMltBG4b7w. In addition to the panelists mentioned in the text above, Tamara Cofman Wittes also participated, and the panel was moderated by James Goldgeier.

Introduction: Why This Book Is for You

Wesley Reisser explains: "I was one of five people in the entire State Department working on LGBTQ issues at all. So I was part of the very tiny vanguard that did it at the start."[1]

Reisser received a PhD in geography, and he has had a distinguished civil service career in the US Department of State. His position in the department positioned him to advance social change much more quickly than he anticipated and on an issue that had deep personal significance. "I consider that my greatest legacy probably that I will ever accomplish at the State Department, was getting LGBTQI issues into the life stream of the UN and making it a real subject within the human rights discussion globally," Reisser told us. "It's been really meaningful because I've also gotten to meet a lot of activists from other countries who have talked about how these mechanisms have given them space to fight for their rights in places that are really, really hard. . . . It's really cool to even say that I'm part of that club of folks who've really got to use the UN to push human rights in new ways."

"There have been times when I have felt compelled to take a step back from my academic research to work on what I felt were more urgent humanitarian and human rights issues," Mara Revkin says, "most recently in 2021, when I took a service leave of absence from my postdoc to work full time for the UN in Baghdad on efforts to repatriate Iraqis, mostly children, from camps and prisons in northeast Syria where they had been stranded since 2019."

Revkin earned her PhD in political science, and, in 2022, she took a faculty position as associate professor at Duke University's School of Law. But committing to work that affects people's lives, especially the lives of vulnerable people, led her to spend significant time during and after her PhD working for the United Nations. "I ended up staying for nine months [in 2021], much longer than planned, because the work felt so much more useful than my academic research. I am back in academia now but still trying to keep one foot in the humanitarian world."

All of us hope in some way to make a difference in the world, as Reisser and Revkin have done. For professors, the primary means of doing so are by producing ideas that change people's understanding of important economic, social, and/or political problems and by expanding the intellectual horizons of new generations. A doctoral program guides students to write a dissertation that adds to human knowledge, and an academic career is driven by the desire to continue adding to human knowledge and broadening understanding. Those interested in a policy career likewise want to make a difference. But they often express their professional goals differently, in terms of effecting concrete societal outcomes.

If you are reading this book, you may already be thinking about getting a PhD, or you may be in the process of getting a PhD; perhaps you have finished your degree and are thinking about what you will do next, or you are working in academia and pondering a career change. You might have known from the beginning that you wanted the advanced degree in pursuit of a career outside academia; maybe you became disillusioned with academia along the way, or perhaps you found when you finished your degree that the academic job market was too restrictive. Or you are just unsure what type of career path you want to pursue, whether in academia or policy. Maybe you pursued a more traditional academic career, and you are looking to take a public service leave for a year or two, or you want to be better able to advise your students as they pursue their lives and careers.

Whatever the reason you picked up this book, we want you to know that there are a wide range of options open to PhDs from a variety of disciplines that allow you to make a difference in the world outside academia if you decide to go down that path with the skills and knowledge you obtained while working toward your degree. As a group of authors from the United States Air Force Academy and the RAND Corporation argue, "Far from being 'lesser' career options, many of these jobs remove the constraints that come with pursuing a tenure-track academic job, allowing you to live where you would like, make more money, influence policy, and give back to your country or community."[2]

In writing this book, we researched more than two dozen career case studies through in-depth interviews with individuals from a range of disciplines, including recent PhDs as well as those at more mid-level and senior stages of their careers. As we learned through our conversations with these professionals, applicants for PhD programs in political science, international relations, history, sociology, and other social science disciplines have myriad reasons to pursue a degree that on average takes five to seven years (depending on the discipline) to complete. Perhaps a professor inspired them or they did an internship in an organization where their mentor possessed a doctorate. They might have done a master's degree and felt there was more they wanted to learn in the classroom, or they believed that a terminal degree would put them in a stronger position for the path they wanted to pursue. They might already have a career in government or the military, and they saw others get a PhD and advance in ways that were attractive to them. Above all, these doctoral students are intellectually curious, and they want to understand the social world and how people interact: how they cooperate, compete, and exercise power. Pursuing a doctoral degree immerses them in theories and methods tested through years of scholarly endeavors to illuminate the social world and enables them to develop deep expertise on Cold War history, the sociology of race, the politics of authoritarian regimes, the role of gender in development, the social impact of emerging technologies, the sources of economic inequalities, and any number of other topics that can entice someone to pursue and complete a PhD.

If you are interested in exploring a policy career, however, you may find it difficult to get the insights and advice you need from within your academic department. When students begin their PhD programs, especially those at major research universities, they are quickly socialized into the pursuit of a tenure-track position at a college or university. There are a number of reasons for this. They are being taught by faculty members who went to graduate school and became professors. Many of these professors have very little experience outside the academy, and most are themselves survivors of a highly competitive and arduous professional gauntlet; they achieved their positions because they valued academia enough to keep going despite the obstacles and odds against securing a permanent faculty position. Departmental rankings are shaped in part by the percentage of students who land tenure-track jobs, particularly at prestigious institutions. If faculty members believe that they and their departments will be measured by their students' success in academia, and thus that their ability to recruit future PhD students is on the line, then they will emphasize the academic job market to those they are training. And aside from the rankings, professors want students who will go into academia to help build the scholarly field in which they are trained and to teach the next generation. The economist Robert Kahn notes that many professors "see themselves as successful to the extent they are generating children in their own image."

PhD programs across the social sciences follow similar templates: the first two years are spent in classes, some of which are focused on theory and methods, with others focused on how to utilize those theories and methods to carry out empirical research. Students can get trained in quantitative and experimental methods (e.g., statistics and survey methods) and/or qualitative methods such as archival and field research. After their coursework is completed, students take oral and/or written comprehensive exams in their areas of specialization, and then they develop a dissertation "prospectus" that lays out the basic idea they want to pursue with their committee. Once their prospectus is approved, they are technically ABD (all but dissertation), and they typically then take the next two or more years to write their dissertation.

During all this time they are in their PhD program, students may wonder about applied careers—specifically, careers as practitioners rather than university-based scholars. But even if that's your outright preference, it can be hard to know how to prepare or where to begin. If you work while in your doctoral program, you are likely either a teaching or research assistant. You may have an interest in making a contribution beyond theoretical and methodological debates in order to produce policy-relevant research, something of increasing interest to PhD students. In fact, a burgeoning number of programs are available to help you pursue these interests, as we describe in later chapters.

This book is for those individuals who want to explore applying their doctoral training to a career in international affairs and foreign policy, whether in the public, private, or nonprofit sectors. You may be considering a career as a practitioner because you like solving certain types of problems. You may be motivated to improve lives and livelihoods or to serve your country or community. Policy work offers the opportunity to leave a professional legacy in local, national, and international communities. Though perhaps you went to graduate school because you were focused on being an academic, you can choose many career paths that suit your personality and where you will find the type of work/life balance you are looking for. How you make those choices will be unique to you. Our goal in writing this book is to encourage you to think broadly about your career opportunities and to offer you guidance on how to pursue applied work in foreign policy.

There are a variety of reasons that PhD holders in history, political science, international affairs, and related fields pursue jobs and careers in foreign policy. The driving motivation for many people is a fundamental desire to pursue public service in government, at an NGO, or with an international organization such as the United Nations. Some may go to graduate school with no intention from the start of seeking a faculty position. Others may initially want to become an academic, only to realize later for intellectual and personal reasons that they would prefer a nonacademic path. They may see the odds of landing a tenure-track job as stacked against them. They may have personal or family reasons to stay tethered to a particular location. They might decide they want to pursue a higher-paying career than is typically found in academia.

This book challenges the idea that "alt-academic" careers, including in policy, are "second-best" outcomes for PhD students. Policy careers can be highly rewarding—intellectually, personally, professionally, emotionally, and financially—in other words, they can be sought after, not settled for. As the Brookings Institution scholar Tanvi Madan says, "Don't think that somebody is in policy because they couldn't cut it in academia or that they're not smart enough." Wesley Reisser reflects: "There's a lot more PhDs than ever before who are practitioners, and jobs in the academy are getting harder. They're both harder to get, and the protections and benefits that come with them are a lot less than used to exist in the past."

The data back up Reisser's observations. At a time when many universities are cutting back on faculty positions, more and more PhDs will be looking for jobs and careers outside academia. A 2013 study showed that even top-ranked political science programs, Harvard and Berkeley, placed fewer than one-fourth of their PhD graduates into tenure-track positions at research universities.[3] In 2015, two-thirds of college professors were adjunct faculty members, possessing little job security and minimal benefits.[4]

In 2020, there were nearly 9,000 doctorate recipients in the United States in psychology and social sciences fields, with another 887 doctorate recipients in history. Nearly 60 percent of those who were employed after receiving doctorates in psychology; 50 percent in economics; about one-third in political science, anthropology, and history; and just over one-fifth in sociology had jobs outside academia in government, nonprofits, and the private sector.[5]

If you have an interest in working in foreign policy, Washington is a huge potential market. But many students simply are not aware of the array of possibilities across the public, private, and nonprofit sectors. We are two academically trained international relations scholars who have spent our careers in Washington, focused on foreign policy, and working in government, in think tanks, and in academia. One of us is a tenured faculty member and former international affairs school dean at a Washington university who helped develop a long-running program that promotes scholarly contributions to policy and public debates;[6] one of us is a career think tanker with experience in government, politics, and the nonprofit sector who helped found an organization that works to improve national security by enabling the elevation of more women to the decision-making table.[7] In our combined fifty years in the field, we have advised dozens, if not hundreds, of graduate students and PhD holders seeking to work in foreign policy careers. We have hired and supervised PhD holders in policy roles both in government and outside it. In this book, we provide well-informed, desperately needed guidance to PhDs seeking fulfilling careers in foreign policy and related areas.

A career in applied policy work does not mean that one needs to forsake academia altogether. There are opportunities to teach as an adjunct professor or even take a leave from your policy job to spend a year or two at a university. Thanks to the proliferation of public policy and international affairs schools and degree programs, there are increasing numbers of opportunities for those who took a nonacademic path in their careers to come back to academia at a later stage to teach, mentor, and publish. And if you do go into the academy, there are a variety of ways to contribute directly to policy, beyond getting people to read your ideas through your writing. These range from advising and consulting to briefing officials, including in the intelligence community, to testifying in front of Congress to working with NGOs and international organizations and to going into government on a public service leave.

This book is targeted primarily to doctoral students and PhD holders in political science, international relations, history, sociology, and the other social sciences, including those working in academia who are interested in pursuing foreign policy careers. Though this book is geared toward students in, or graduates of, United States–based doctoral programs who are interested in pursuing policy careers in Washington, our advice will also be relevant to those interested in private-sector jobs in Silicon Valley, international organization opportunities in cities like New York and Geneva, and policy jobs in local domestic or overseas communities. But this book does not consider the full range of nonacademic career paths available to social science PhD holders. We are focused on advising people who want to make a difference by informing, shaping, deciding, implementing, and evaluating policies in the world of governments and the institutions and communities that surround, support, and interact with them.

The chapters that follow illuminate what foreign policy careers can look like, the range of organizations that are part of the "foreign policy ecosystem," how to decide what kind of policy work might fit your passions and skills, and how to pursue a job in foreign policy. Along the way, we lay out some of the delights and dilemmas that you are likely to find before you if you choose a career in applied work. We hope that this book also provides a ready resource for academic advisers whose students express interest in nonacademic careers. And, by offering insights into the full array of foreign policy–focused organizations and examples of career trajectories, we also address this book to those already working in policy who want to explore broader career options.[8]

In the chapters that follow, we explain the differences between working *on* foreign policy and working *in* foreign policy. We examine the different types of work environments and organizational structures one encounters in foreign policy, to help you explore your motivations and work styles, so you can hone your job search to the right kinds of work for you. While most academics think of a policy career as working either in government or in think tanks, this book reveals the wide array of organizations and environments you can be part of when doing foreign policy: the executive and legislative branches of the US government; think tanks; direct service organizations; issue advocacy organizations; philanthropic foundations; corporate, consulting, and lobbying firms; and journalism. Finally, the book will help you navigate the policy community and better understand how to build your networks and present your skills and expertise in order to find receptive audiences for your work.

Along the way, you will meet a diverse group of individuals with doctoral degrees who have pursued policy-focused careers in different places and who are at different stages of their professional lives. We spoke with more than two dozen individuals across the government, nonprofit, and private sectors in preparing this guidebook. Throughout the book, we share their insights with you, and we offer illustrative profiles of individuals working in a range of foreign policy careers to provide you with models and inspiration.

We hope that in the pages that follow, you will discover your own way to create a rewarding career path applying your expertise and skills to a career in foreign policy.

Box I.1. Policy Professionals and Others Interviewed for This Book

The positions listed were those held at the time this book was written.

Mary Barton, PhD in history, University of Virginia, and analyst, US government

Paul J. Bonicelli, PhD in political science, University of Tennessee, and senior policy adviser to US senator Rick Scott

Reuben Brigety, DPhil in international relations, Cambridge University, and US ambassador to the Republic of South Africa

Susanna Campbell, PhD in international relations, Fletcher School at Tufts University, and associate professor at American University

Ivo Daalder, PhD in political science, Massachusetts Institute of Technology, and president, Chicago Council for Global Affairs

Zoe Danon, PhD in politics, Brandeis University, and coordinator of research planning, Foreign Affairs, Defense, and Trade Division, Congressional Research Service

Stephen Del Rosso, PhD in political science, University of Pennsylvania, and program director, International Peace and Security, Carnegie Corporation of New York

Erik Durbin, PhD in economics, Columbia University, and section chief, consumer household research and policy, Consumer Financial Protection Bureau

Alexandra Evans, PhD in history, University of Virginia, and associate policy researcher, RAND Corporation

Alice Hunt Friend, PhD in international service, American University, and vice president for research and analysis, Institute for Security and Technology

Steve Galpern, PhD in history, University of Texas, and acting director, Office of Near Eastern Affairs, Bureau of Intelligence and Research, US Department of State

Matthew Jacobs, PhD in history, Ohio University, and briefer, President's Daily Brief Staff, Office of the Director of National Intelligence

Robert Kahn, PhD in economics, Massachusetts Institute of Technology, and director, global macroeconomics, Eurasia Group

Morgan Kaplan, PhD in political science, University of Chicago, and former executive editor, *International Security*

Kristin Lord, PhD in government, Georgetown University, and president of International Research and Exchange (IREX)

Tanvi Madan, PhD in public policy, University of Texas, and senior fellow and director of the India Project, Brookings Institution

Jennifer McArdle, PhD in war studies, Kings College, and head of research at Improbable

Paul McLachlan, PhD in political science, University of California, San Diego, and senior engineering manager, core battery data, at Rivian

Sara Plana, PhD in political science, Massachusetts Institute of Technology, and senior intelligence assistant to the undersecretary of defense for intelligence and security

Barry Posen, PhD in political science, University of California, Berkeley, and director emeritus, Security Studies Program, and Ford International Professor of Political Science at Massachusetts Institute of Technology

Dafna Rand, PhD in political science, Columbia University, and director of the Office of Foreign Assistance at US Department of State

Wesley Reisser, PhD in geography, University of California, Los Angeles, and deputy director of the Office of Human Rights and Humanitarian Affairs in the Bureau of International Organizations, US Department of State

Mara Revkin, PhD in political science, Yale University, and associate professor at Duke University School of Law

Susan Rice, DPhil in international relations, Oxford University, and assistant to the president for domestic policy and director of the Domestic Policy Council, White House
Carla Anne Robbins, PhD in political science, University of California, Berkeley, and director of the Master's in International Affairs Program at Marxe School of Public and International Affairs, Baruch College
Jon Rosenwasser, PhD in international relations, Fletcher School at Tufts University, and budget and policy director at Select Committee on Intelligence, US Senate
William Ruger, PhD in politics, Brandeis University, and president, American Institute for Economic Research
Kori Schake, PhD in government and politics, University of Maryland, and senior fellow and director of foreign and defense policy studies, American Enterprise Institute
Erin Simpson, PhD in government, Harvard University, and senior adviser on industrial base policy at US Department of Defense
James Graham Wilson, PhD in history, University of Virginia, and supervisory historian, Global Issues and General Division, Office of the Historian, US Department of State
Rebecca Wolfe, PhD in social psychology, Harvard University, and senior lecturer, Harris School of Public Policy at University of Chicago

Notes

1. Any quotations in the book without a direct citation come from the conversations we had with the individuals listed at the end of this introduction in box I.1.

2. Danielle Gilbert, S. R. Gubitz, Jennifer Kavanagh, and Kelly Piazza, "Pushing the Boundaries of Your PhD: Exploring Careers outside the Ivory Tower," APSA Preprints, doi: 10.33774/apsa-2022-cr3fz.

3. Scott Jaschik, "Poli Sci Professor Producers," *Inside Higher Ed*, September 3, 2013, https://www.insidehighered.com/news/2013/09/03/study-examines-trends-phd-programs-produce-political-science-professors.

4. Caroline Fredrickson, "There Is No Excuse for How Universities Treat Adjuncts," *Atlantic*, September 15, 2015, https://www.theatlantic.com/business/archive/2015/09/higher-education-college-adjunct-professor-salary/404461/.

5. National Science Foundation, "Survey of Earned Doctorates," no date, https://ncses.nsf.gov/pubs/nsf22300/data-tables#group7, tables 63 and 67.

6. Bridging the Gap, https://bridgingthegapproject.org/.

7. Leadership Council for Women in National Security, "Celebrating Women's Leadership and Helping Them Succeed," no date, https://www.lcwins.org/.

8. Other books that discuss careers outside of academia include Christopher L. Caterine, *Leaving Academia: A Practical Guide* (Princeton, NJ: Princeton University Press, 2020); Susan Elizabeth Basalla and Maggie Debelius, *"So What Are You Going to Do with That? Finding Careers outside Academia*, 3rd ed. (Chicago: University of Chicago Press, 2015); Joseph Fruscione and Kelly J. Baker, *Succeeding outside the Academy: Career Paths beyond the Humanities, Social Sciences, and STEM*

(Lawrence: University Press of Kansas, 2018); and Derick W. Brinkerhoff and Jennifer M. Brinkerhoff, *Working for Change: Making a Career in International Public Service* (Hartford: Kumarian Press, 2005). You might also find inspiring books by PhDs who made their careers outside academia, such as an individual with whom we spoke, Ambassador Susan Rice, who tells her personal story in *Tough Love: My Story of the Things Worth Fighting For* (New York: Simon & Schuster, 2019).

1

Working *in* Foreign Policy versus Working *on* Foreign Policy

You may have entered your doctoral program knowing you wanted a policy career, as one of us did. You may have aspired to a professorial career but may have determined for any of a variety of reasons that it wasn't right for you. Most of the available guidance for doctoral students and graduates about careers outside academia treats these careers as a fallback, as evidenced by guidebook titles like *Leaving Academia*.[1] This book treats foreign policy careers differently—as a professional path that applies advanced social science training to address important policy questions and solve practical problems. More and more academics also seek to do this through their scholarly contributions; a practitioner is typically engaging more directly in problem-solving or in some cases conducting research and writing in response to a direct request from policymakers. Just as engineering is no less legitimate a career path than researching theoretical physics, applied social science is no more or less legitimate a way to use one's doctoral training than theoretical social science. It simply treats a different problem set, and it envisions making an impact in different ways.

Nearly all social science disciplines, and many liberal arts disciplines as well, such as history and law, train students to evaluate arguments and evidence using a set of well-honed theoretical frameworks and methodological tools. They teach a rigorous approach to causal inference, enabling post facto analysis as well as prediction. This is the core skill set of policy work as well. As the field of political science has documented, too many policymakers undertake these essential evaluative tasks without sufficient rigor, influenced instead by rules of thumb, bureaucratic interests, groupthink, and a variety of other cognitive and organizational biases.[2]

Those with formal training through a doctoral degree thus have valuable skills to improve the rigor and reliability of policy analysis, policy debates, policy decisions, and thus, one hopes, to improve outcomes. Indeed, many policy institutions are sensitive to the need to improve the rigor of their work, and bringing in talent with doctoral-level training is a key component of their strategy to do so. As you'll see later in this book, doctoral graduates are working in the Defense Department, international development agencies, humanitarian organizations, human rights advocacy groups, and many other places, making a meaningful difference in the quality and impact of these institutions' efforts. These institutions view PhD holders not as "failed academics" but as researchers with an interest in applied questions who bring uniquely valuable skills and expertise to the world of foreign policy.

Many people have very successful careers in policy without holding a PhD. Many possess a master's degree and/or a JD. But as we will see, a doctorate can make you a more attractive candidate, whether entering government for a career or seeking to take a leave from academia for a public service opportunity.

If you are finishing up your PhD or hold a postdoctoral fellowship, you are already accustomed to working long hours by yourself, over a long period, focused on a single big project. You are likely using that project to ask and answer questions that respond to theoretical and/or methodological debates in your academic field of study. Policy work can also involve long hours, but most policy work is different from graduate school and academic research along dimensions that include the nature of the work environment, time frame, audience, scope, and impact. This chapter explains some of the ways in which applied work in foreign policy differs from academic knowledge building in fields like history, international relations, and area studies.

Analysis for Policy Applications: Different Goals Lead to Different Questions

In practice, a policy analyst, like an academic, uses the theories and methods—that is, the disciplinary approaches—that you learned or are learning in your graduate studies to examine, understand, evaluate, and propose answers to social science questions. But the nature of the questions you will ask in a policy career are often very different from the questions you might ask in academic scholarship. In international relations, for example, an academic might ask, How do democratic leaders evaluate the risk of military casualties in making the decision to go to war? And what does this tell us about the interaction between domestic politics and foreign policy? The academic is concerned with gaining insights to enhance the general understanding of decision-making. The policy analyst, by contrast, is usually concerned with a specific case or application of general insights. A policy question on the same issue might be formulated as, How will the risk of military casualties affect the president's calculation to go to war right now? More pointedly, an adviser to that president might ask, Given the level of risk of military casualties, will it harm the president politically if he or she chooses to go to war in this instance, and what will I advise him or her when we meet?

Answering an applied question requires understanding the state of general knowledge about democratic decision-making and military casualties, just as answering an academic question might. But this understanding is not designed for—nor is it sufficient to predict, advise, or decide on—a given path or outcome in a specific context. Like many academics, the policy analyst will have not just the general theory and disciplinary methodology to guide their work but also expertise regarding the specific context, actors, and history. Academics can always choose another question if the data lead them in a different direction than they were planning to go. Policy analysts are typically responding to a specific question or what is known as a "tasking" in the policy world; they don't have the option to pick a different question to answer.

Academics are usually reluctant to make predictions about a specific case based on the generalized knowledge they have built. Their findings are often nuanced and contingent. They might, for example, be able to describe the likeliest way that civil wars end, given a certain set of variables. A policy professional, meanwhile, is focused on a particular civil war and whether and how it might be brought to a conclusion. Academic analysis on likely outcomes can be informative, but often it is not specific enough to be prescriptive for any single case a policymaker is deliberating. This is why the late Stanford political scientist Alexander George and his colleagues argued in favor of academics developing contingent generalizations about specific types of international problems such as deterrence and coercive diplomacy.[3] In going from academia to policy, an individual needs to go from academic findings for contingent generalizations that can provide guidance in a particular case through the knowledge gained from past cases to actually providing concrete advice to superiors about what to do in a given situation.

As noted above, the difference between academic social science and applied social science, then, is not unlike the difference between physics or chemistry lab research and physical or chemical engineering. For instance, a physicist can offer you well-tested and reliable information about the tolerances of different types of metals in different configurations. But to determine what metals are or aren't well suited to a given building project, and certainly to design and construct the project itself, you will want to hire an experienced building engineer.

In thinking about whether a policy career makes sense for you, it's worth considering what kinds of research questions you have found most engaging through the course of your academic work. Many PhD students are trained to answer research questions that will make a theoretical or methodological contribution that will be valued by other scholars. That's important, but in a different way from more policy-focused research. It's certainly the case that even more academically focused work can make contributions to policy over the long run. As the Carnegie Corporation of New York's Stephen Del Rosso has written, "A classic example is Swedish Nobel laureate Gunnar Myrdal's 1944 study of race relations, *The American Dilemma*, which was largely ignored and even disavowed by its sponsors for over a decade until it proved essential to the landmark Supreme Court decision in *Brown v. Board of Education*."[4]

In general, however, those who gravitate toward policy tend to do so because they want to work on something different from more classic disciplinary scholarship. Dafna Rand, who is currently working in a senior position at the Department of State, recalls being surprised that, when entering her doctoral program and meeting her peers, she "began to see that we were set to very different meters of what we were interested in." If you don't find the questions you're working on compelling, you are unlikely to enjoy the work necessary to answer them. It's really a matter of taste, and you will want to figure out where your tastes run. Says Kori Schake, who leads the foreign policy and defense program at the American Enterprise Institute, "I wouldn't have chosen it [an academic career]. . . . I wouldn't have prospered at it in a way I have prospered in applied work, because it's the questions that make policy work such fun."

What questions do you find most fun to work on? Are they centered more on theoretical and/or methodological debates? Or are you eager to solve pressing policy questions? Understanding your preferences will help you figure out what kind of work will help you thrive. Though there are plenty of scholars who want to solve puzzles that have positive spillover effects on society, they don't get many opportunities to implement policies unless they take a public service leave from a government job. The closest they might otherwise come is briefing or consulting with policymakers. Rand and Schake found policy questions more interesting than theoretical or methodological ones; you might be the opposite. Figuring out which you prefer is what's most important.

Constraints in Policy Analysis

As the examples given above suggest, the scope of applied policy questions is typically quite different from the scope of scholarly questions: whereas academic research seeks to produce generalizable insights, policy questions typically relate to a specific case in a specific context and time frame. Both can be theoretically informed, but answering the policy question demands accounting for that specificity with an explanation or a solution that will work in the existing context. That context is likely to include limited time, limited resources, and limited information. In policy work, as when stranded on a desert island with only canned food, you cannot simply, as the old economists' joke suggests, assume a can opener.

The time frame for examining policy questions is typically shorter than that available for academic investigations. When your goal is to add reliable insights to the store of human knowledge, you can take years to collect evidence through fieldwork or by assembling databases and take years more to draft, present, solicit feedback, refine, and publish your work. By contrast, time constraints are inherent to policy work, and indeed some degree of urgency is a common component.

Policy work also operates within the constraints of available resources, including funding, staffing, technological and other capacity limits, and of course the will of leaders, politicians, and the public to sustain certain policy paths. Effective policy analysis need not always limit itself to match these constraints—indeed, it is often important to make clear to both policymakers and the public that there is no way to achieve certain goals without altering the structure of the environment or the inputs committed to the effort. There are also times when a policy analyst can construct a solution to a long-standing problem, but this solution cannot win sufficient support at the time it is rolled out—instead, presenting and marketing the solution itself can help to galvanize political will and secure the needed resources to make the solution viable. Sometimes, a policy solution may be available in principle, but it must wait for implementation until the political stars align behind it. These elements of context are not within the policy analyst's control, and they cannot be "controlled for" in analysis. Instead, they must be observed, examined to determine whether they are "hard" or "soft" constraints, and then appropriately factored into the analysis. In this way, policy analysis is like household budgeting for a growing family—the variables are shifting as you undertake the analysis, and your planning assumptions must be regularly revisited.

A final and essential component of the policy context is that you almost never know everything you need to know in order to undertake a full analysis and prescription of the challenge before you. The data available to investigate policy questions are often murky and/or incomplete; available information may come from sources whose reliability cannot be assumed or must be subjected to cross-checking and vetting (this type of intelligence analysis is its own policy analysis specialty). Policy analysis demands the ability to push past uncertainty to arrive at the best available, and sometimes the least worst, option to answer time-sensitive questions.

This aspect of policy analysis can make trained social scientists uncomfortable since social science knowledge building rests on our embrace of contingent knowledge that must be constantly tested, challenged, and amended. Making real-world policy recommendations or decisions based on imperfect and contingent knowledge can feel unethical or at least discomfiting. A degree of comfort with uncertainty and a willingness to proffer ideas and make recommendations or decisions despite uncertainty is inherent to policy work. Kristin Lord relates an experience from her first policy role, at the State Department: "I was working on Internet freedom and I wrote up this paper and I handed it to a principal, and the person said, 'This is brilliant. I agree with everything that you've written.' And then put it down and said, 'What would you like me to do about it?' And I was caught completely flat footed, I could not answer, did not understand, because you never do that in academia. You never learn what are the levers you can pull to actually do things."

At the end of the day, policy workers are problem solvers. Creativity, and the ability to MacGyver a fix on occasion, can be central to success.

The Policy Workplace Is Its Own Context

One of the most notable aspects of working in the policy arena is that external factors dictate much of what you do. For many people, one of academia's greatest attractions is the freedom to set your own research agenda and determine your own schedule for research and writing; in policy, this freedom is largely absent. Even in the think tank sector, research agendas must be responsive to the questions that are considered important to the think tank's key audiences in government, the media, philanthropy, and the private sector—and, potentially, to a think tank's funders. The "so what" question that doctoral students are trained to answer about their dissertation means something different in policy work, and it looms much larger. For academics, "so what" usually refers to answering a question that makes an important theoretical or methodological contribution. Relevance to policy problems is often not a requirement for a dissertation. A policy analyst is responding to questions that are top of mind to decision-makers; you cannot succeed without being able to demonstrate and communicate the relevance of your work to those with the power to make decisions.

Let's take the example of NATO's adaptation after the end of the Cold War. NATO was an institution designed to counter the threat posed by the Soviet Union to Western Europe, so it faced questions about its relevance when the USSR collapsed at the end of 1991. Academics asked what might happen to NATO and gave different answers depending on their theoretical perspective. Some argued that an alliance is formed against specific threats, so when these threats disappear, so does the alliance, and that's what we could expect of NATO.[5] Others argued from an institutionalist or identity perspective that the organization would find new missions to keep it in business.[6]

Policymakers who believed in the importance of NATO for American national interests and European security might be interested in the theoretical debates, but they would be more eager for a specific analysis of how different actors in and around NATO would address the question of its future and for specific recommendations regarding what it could and should do over time. Prior training in academia could help with the general framing of the problem, but someone working in policy would want to develop actionable items that governments and NATO itself could implement as it adapted to a new environment. And in policy, as in academic administration, there are also always bureaucratic interests shaping the conversation.[7]

Writing for a policy audience also means that you cannot, as academic researchers might, isolate and analyze just one variable to explain its importance; policy analysis demands multivariate, multilevel analysis. Tanvi Madan notes, "You don't just make policy in one stream. . . . With the Kyoto agreement, you just don't think about climate change; you have to think about corporations. You have to think about domestic politics."

For academics, communication skills are essential—for teaching and for sharing your work with peers, students, and wider audiences. In academia, your primary audience is other scholars who work on similar questions. This means that academic writing may focus as much on *how* you got the answer to a question as on *what* the answer is. Academic communication often employs shorthand or jargon to make information sharing more efficient among a community of experts. The focus on knowledge generation and knowledge sharing among peers can be so strong that academic professionals sometimes dismiss research areas that appear less likely to contribute generalizable knowledge for the field or devalue activities designed to bring a scholar's ideas to a general audience, such as trade press books, op-eds, and television appearances. And yet, because of their teaching experience, many academics are skilled at communicating complex ideas in terms easy for wider audiences to understand.

For policy workers, strong oral and written communication skills are essential. The press of time and attention among senior policymakers and those implementing policy in the field demands that you share insights briefly and clearly. Though nuances and complexity are inevitable, and important, you must also translate complex and nuanced insights into actionable proposals.

Most of all, policy communication is tightly focused on, and varies by, its audience. Good policy communication holds the attention and meets the needs of very specific audiences. For instance, for an analyst at the National Intelligence Council, this audience may be the president of the United States. For a State Department diplomat, the audience may be a foreign official weighing whether to accede to a US request, a colleague who might support or oppose you in an interagency policy debate, or a Capitol Hill staff member who is weighing your funding request. For a congressional staff member, the audience may be other members of your senator's committee. For a program officer at the National Democratic Institute, the audience may be a grants officer at the US Agency for International Development or a civil society activist in the country where you work. For a think tank scholar, the audience may be a Sunday talk show host, newspaper editorial writer, senior government official, or midlevel officer in a combatant command whom you get the opportunity to brief. The form and substance of your policy communication must be finely tuned to address your desired audience in the way most likely to meet their needs, answer their questions, and influence their thinking.

Most policy work, although not all, takes place in larger organizations, where the analysis and action undertaken serve a shared organizational mission. This sense of common purpose, whether to advance the public interest or end global poverty or pass legislation or create a better product, is often a highly motivating feature of the professional experience for policy workers. But working in a large organization as part of a team contributing to a shared mission also means working within the organization's hierarchy and its often-frustrating bureaucracy. Especially in government, the process of creating policy analysis and recommendations is designed to ensure that all stakeholders have a chance to weigh in on the work product, and that all possible good options are surfaced and considered, before decisions are made. You may think you have written a brilliant document, only to wonder what happened to all your great ideas and sentences after the memo has gone through the process of being "cleared" by all the individuals involved in the process who have what are called "equities"—that is, a stake in the outcome. This can lead to slow and painstaking progress and to a day-to-day work experience that puts a premium on interpersonal skills and consensus building, sometimes at the expense of analytical clarity or innovative ideas.

Also, of course, working on policy within a large organization on behalf of a shared mission means having a boss who shapes what you do, when, and how. Often, you will have many layers of bosses. "Managing up" may be one of the biggest challenges you will face if you go into a policy job. Sure, you've had a dissertation supervisor; but in academia, you are largely working on your own projects at your own pace and are producing your own work. In a policy job, you are often responding to multiple demands from your boss (who may have gotten the demands from their boss), working as part of a team to respond, and doing so in the time frame you have been given. For a manager, working in a group setting may require a new set of skills; it certainly requires some adaptability from the isolation of PhD research and writing. Conversely, having a close and immediate connection between your daily work and the person or people who will make use of it can be very fulfilling. Indeed, some policy jobs are focused on staffing a principal—that is, giving your senior official the background, analysis, advice, and support they need to do their job effectively and accompanying them through their activities. For many people, enabling the success of a senior leader of character, learning from someone with the capacity to truly drive events, is a career highlight. In any event, your boss in a policy job is probably the person with the greatest ability to make your work joyful or miserable, so we advise you to choose your bosses carefully! (The same will hold true if you go into academic administration.) Michèle Flournoy, who served as undersecretary of defense for policy under President Barack Obama, has famously said, "Choose the boss, not the job."[8] You can't always do that, but they are definitely words to remember as you progress in your career.

From Analysis to Action: Policy Work in Practice

Two additional distinctions between academic analysis and policy analysis are worth considering, and we will return to them later in this book. First, policy analysis demands not simply that you diagnose and build understanding about a problem or set of problems; to have an impact, you must consider (and in some environments, propose, evaluate, debate, decide on, and/or implement) real-world *solutions* that take account of your understanding. The second key difference is the role of normative judgments: your policy solutions will be decided and acted on by particular actors with their own interests, resources, power, and legitimacy (whether individual leaders, parliaments, international organizations, corporations, civil society groups, or other actors). Thus, your solutions cannot escape normative questions about what "should" happen or what your decision-makers "should" do next. One of the hardest lessons for some policymakers to learn is that the Hippocratic principle of doing no harm is almost impossible to implement in foreign policy, especially for a country whose interests and influence are as diverse and globe spanning as the United States. Even if there is no great answer to a problem, the bureaucracy often must come up with *an* answer. And choosing not to act in a given circumstance can have practical and moral consequences, in some cases for hundreds of thousands or millions of people.

Some policy careers are, like academia, focused on asking and answering analytical questions. But the policy arena includes a wide array of roles that go beyond analytical work to debating policy options; making decisions; implementing policy through diplomacy, projects, and other activity; and evaluating or overseeing actors and outcomes. All these components of the policy world offer exciting and challenging career opportunities—and they all benefit from the expertise, insight, and analytical rigor that one acquires through a successful doctoral education. The next chapter will help you explore how you like to work, the different environments policy work can offer, and what types of policy jobs different personal preferences might suggest for you.

Notes

1. Christopher L. Caterine, *Leaving Academia: A Practical Guide* (Princeton, NJ: Princeton University Press, 2020).

2. The classic work on these issues is by Robert Jervis, *Perception and Misperception in International Politics* (Princeton, NJ: Princeton University Press, 1976).

3. Alexander L. George and Richard Smoke, *Deterrence in American Foreign Policy: Theory and Practice* (New York: Columbia University Press, 1974); Alexander L. George, David K. Hall, and William E. Simons, *The Limits of Coercive Diplomacy* (Boston: Little, Brown, 1971).

4. Stephen J. Del Rosso, "Our New Three Rs: Rigor, Relevance, and Readability," *Governance* 28, no. 2 (2015): 130.

5. As Kenneth Waltz argued in 1993, "NATO's days are not numbered, but its years are." Kenneth N. Waltz, "The Emerging Structure of International Politics," *International Security* 18, no. 2 (Fall 1993): 76.

6. See, e.g., Celeste A. Wallander, "Institutional Assets and Adaptability: NATO after the Cold War," *International Organization* 54, no. 4 (2000): 705–35.

7. On the bureaucratic interests involved in the debate within the US government on NATO enlargement in the 1990s, e.g., see James M. Goldgeier, *Not Whether but When: The US Decision to Enlarge NATO* (Washington, DC: Brookings Institution Press, 1999).

8. Council on Foreign Relations, "Life Lessons Learned with Michèle Flournoy," webinar, June 10, 2021, https://www.cfr.org/event/life-lessons-learned-michele -flournoy.

2

Creating Opportunities in Graduate School

If you are pursuing a PhD, you clearly love learning, being in school, and getting the opportunity to do in-depth research. You might be pretty certain that you want to be a professor, or pretty certain that you don't, but you might be seeking more information on how you can make the most of your time in graduate school to set yourself up for different types of careers.

And what if you haven't started a PhD yet but are merely considering it? Should you do it? As we will see, a number of people we spoke with pursued the degree because they wanted the credential or just because it was something they had their heart set on doing.

As a Fletcher School professor, Daniel Drezner, has written, it is a lot easier to start a PhD than it is to finish it. "What separates a PhD from other degrees," he argues, "is the scholarly act of writing a dissertation. If there is no genuine fascination with the subject matter, if there is no love of the topic, then there is a 99.5 percent probability of failure. That has to be the primary driver. If it's fame and fortune, then the professional degree route—a JD, an MBA, or a MALD—is the better route for you."[1] Or as Wesley Reisser, who received his PhD in geography, puts it, "Nobody gets a PhD because it's the thing you need to do, but because it's a labor of love."[2]

One thing you might consider if you haven't started a program yet and think you might be interested in policy is to try to find a foreign policy internship or job in Washington for a year or two to start building your network. Morgan Kaplan went to graduate school straight from his undergraduate education, so it was easy for him to be socialized quickly into the idea that he was in a PhD program to become an academic, even though that wasn't the reason he pursued the degree initially. Success in his program, as in most programs, was "defined in academic terms." He adds, "Despite my connections to the policy world, after three years of graduate school, you just totally forget that there's anything else out there but academia." Once you are enrolled in a PhD program, see if your university has a DC center (if your main campus isn't already located there). Many universities do have such centers, and you could offer to TA or even teach your own class there to help build the kind of networks we will be discussing in this chapter.

Do You *Need* a PhD?

If you decided to get a PhD because you love school and didn't have another plan, you are not alone. Nearly every person we spoke with for this book had only a vague idea when they started their degree what they were going to do with their PhD. As Kristin Lord, the president of IREX, told us, "when a professor of mine said I should consider applying to a PhD program, I thought he might as well have said, have you ever considered being an astronaut, because it had never crossed my mind, I didn't know anyone with a PhD except for my professors. And I honestly was very poorly informed about PhDs, what a PhD entailed. Now, I'm very happy I didn't know that because I probably would never have done it. And I am glad I did it. But I was very poorly informed."

For some, the PhD was an obvious path because they knew they loved school and they couldn't think of anything else to do. Kori Schake—who went on to have a distinguished career at the Pentagon, State Department, and White House, and then served in leadership positions at the International Institute for Strategic Studies and the American Enterprise Institute—recalls, "When I graduated from college, I didn't have a plan, so I thought I'd just stay in school because I'm good at school. And I thought I was going to write a PhD about the renaissance of the novel in Latin America in the 1970s, . . . by which I mean to say, I had no career path."

Ivo Daalder—who became a think tank scholar, US ambassador to NATO, and the president of the Chicago Council on Global

Affairs—had a ready-made model for the PhD in his father, a renowned political scientist. But he knew he didn't want to be an academic. "I did a PhD because I had no idea what else I wanted to do." But while he went to graduate school, it was not to replicate his father's career: "The last thing I wanted to do was to be an academic; that wasn't what I wanted to do, which is why everything I did was highly policy relevant. So, I was always on the policy side."

Mary Barton, who received a PhD in history from the University of Virginia and now works as an analyst for the US government, says, "I really loved history in school, and later pursuing a PhD gave me direction and a path forward." Getting the degree, she says, "wasn't because I wanted to have that title in my career. It was because I wanted to study history, and I had a passion for it."

Perhaps you want a PhD because you want to be known as an, if not *the*, expert in a given area. Dafna Rand—who has worked at the State Department and on the National Security Council staff, in addition to building the research team in Mercy Corps' policy office—says, "I was increasingly convinced that a master's would not set me apart. . . . I saw [when working on Capitol Hill] how intellectual expertise, deep substantive expertise, could be very valuable—and I decided I wanted to be the expert in the room." Mara Revkin was a junior researcher at two think tanks in DC before pursuing a JD and a PhD at Yale. Both during and after graduate school, she worked as a researcher and adviser to United Nations agencies on humanitarian and peacebuilding issues in Iraq and Syria. She recalls, "I got to a point in DC where I loved the work, and it was a fascinating time to be working on the Arab Spring, but you do quickly hit a ceiling in DC with what you can do without a master's or an advanced degree."

It's clear from our interviews that, especially for those who come from backgrounds that are underrepresented or marginalized in the policy world, a PhD offers an additional credential and a reason to be taken seriously. This may be especially true for foreign policy and national security. As Kori Schake put it, "24-year-old me, 26-year-old me, and even 30-year-old me, it made me more confident in my own contributions to be Dr. Schake." Alice Hunt Friend, who pursued her PhD at American University, found the same thing to be true. She put it bluntly: "Being called a Dr. was a huge leg up. Especially since I am female, and I also look at least 10 years younger than I really am." Susan Rice, who has served in multiple Cabinet-level positions, says of her early career, "Being a young Black woman, if I weren't Dr. Rice, I think it would have been quite a bit harder." Tanvi Madan, who emigrated from India, did her PhD in public policy at the University of Texas at Austin, and is now a senior fellow at the Brookings Institution, states, "For me especially as an international student at that time, the [career] options were limited. . . . I think whether or not I was in India or America or France, I needed to get a PhD. Especially as a young woman, . . . I realized, look, I'm not going to be able to go and get government experience."

Our interviews also make clear that the PhD was not simply a credential for these women but also something they wanted for themselves. Dr. Friend says that during her first year in her program, still uncertain about where it would lead her, she just decided, "I just want the training, I want it for myself, I don't want it to qualify for something. I just want it because I want it, because when I die, I want to know I have this." If it's something you want to do, then getting the degree provides an intangible that cannot be measured. American University professor Susanna Campbell decided to pursue a PhD after establishing herself in a career working in NGOs and international organizations, and after finishing her degree, she took up a postdoc in Geneva before landing a tenure-track faculty position in Washington. It wasn't easy leaving a management-level position at the United Nations that she had achieved in her mid-twenties, but, she reflects, "I just kind of realized that the depth of exploration and analysis that I was looking for was not going to be found within the UN, that there just wasn't that kind of space for that thinking; . . . for me it was a gradual realization that who I was, how my brain worked, and how I wanted to contribute to the world was going to require a PhD because I was motivated by a fundamental curiosity and need to understand." Now a tenured professor, Campbell has established the Research on International Policy Implementation Lab (RIPIL), affiliated with the Bridging the Gap initiative. RIPIL "creates partnerships among researchers, policymakers, and practitioners to identify important research questions, conduct rigorous research on these questions, and engage policymakers and practitioners throughout the research process."[3]

If you love research and writing, and you are intellectually curious, you'll probably find that a PhD program is a good fit for you. If it's what you really want to do, then you're probably going to do it even if others advise you not to. And if you are like most people, you will pursue the degree without knowing whether you really want to be a professor or even whether there is a job out there for you if you do. You might have been working in a policy job, like Susanna Campbell, and decide you want to leave to pursue the degree. Or you might be working in the public or nonprofit sector and decide to do a PhD simultaneously, as Wesley Reisser, Stephen Del Rosso, and Alice Hunt Friend did (not an easy path!). Or you might just have a vague notion that you could be interested in policy, and you want to get the degree to deepen, and credential, your expertise. Or you might just want to get the degree because you get it in your head that you want to get a PhD, even if you don't know what you want to do with it.

Even once you've gotten the PhD, you still may not know what you want to do with it, and you may pursue any number of options during your career as you follow your passions. Morgan Kaplan finished writing his dissertation on a predoctoral fellowship at the Stanford University Center for International Security and Cooperation, and then he took up a postdoctoral fellowship at the Belfer Center at the Harvard Kennedy School. It was at the Kennedy School where he "drank what felt like DC water again," and he began thinking again about nonfaculty careers. He was subsequently awarded another postdoc at Northwestern University, but after unsuccessfully interviewing for a couple of tenure-track positions, he decided that he was leaving the academic job market.

Kaplan says his experience navigating the job market since then (as the editor of *International Security*, a think tank scholar, and now working in the private sector) has been a roller coaster that he thinks more people should understand: "You go through cycles of first anxiety about what you don't want, followed by excitement over opportunities that are out there, and then back to feeling overwhelmed by all the different possible career paths. That cycle of emotions repeats over and over again." He reminds us that "any job market is hard. Frustration, excitement, stress, and then it's rinse and repeat. But recognizing that this cycle exists helped regulate both the highs and the lows."

The Advantages of a PhD in Policy Work

Our interviews suggest that getting a doctoral degree can confer at least four advantages on policy workers: it teaches them how to formulate good questions, it trains them in rigorous evaluation of causality, it guides them in evaluating data and their implications for decision-making, and it demonstrates that they have persistence and commitment to their chosen issue area and/or expertise on a given country or region.

Although the policy world emphasizes the ability to make decisions and act on them, having individuals who know how to ask questions can prove quite valuable. Different disciplines have different requirements for the PhD dissertation. Some disciplines, like history and certain subfields of political science, focus on producing book-length manuscripts. Others, such as economics, are more focused on writing a set of articles. Either way, students learn how to probe and prod, never accepting assumptions but always questioning them to produce better theories of how the world works. Wesley Reisser reflects, "In grad school, you're given abilities, especially in a doctoral program, to learn to think of things at more levels and to question a lot of assumptions that we're trained about through high school, undergraduate school, and a master's program. And then you finally deconstruct a lot of those, where they come from, at the doctoral level, and not until then. And that ability to question things on multiple layers is really important, because a lot of our policy breakdowns happen because we just sort of accept where things are and try to build or keep the train moving in the same direction without asking questions and thinking about where we need to turn a corner."

Alice Hunt Friend adds, "What has been so helpful about the PhD in the policy world is the ability to have clarity of thought. In the policy world, especially the defense policy world, there's just a lot of muddled and rushed thinking. People don't know when they're making assumptions, and they don't know when and whether to identify their assumptions and challenge them. Even in the deliberate planning world where that's a clear step, telling the difference between an assumption and a variable, for example, if you are not well trained in it, you can't recognize those things. I think being able to think problems through and also being able to recognize really bad analysis when you see it, which is everywhere."

Even as she finished up her PhD at MIT and began to pursue her career, Sara Plana understood, "A lot of policy is based on causal assumptions. How you can approximate, in a world of poor data, the kind of data you would need to judge alternative explanations. . . . Now that I've been indoctrinated into that way of systematic thinking, I see it everywhere." Dafna Rand learned from her work on the Senate Select Committee on Intelligence's Study of the Central Intelligence Agency's Detention and Interrogation Program how important "causality thinking" is to policy: "This notion that you're trained as an academic to think about the causal impact of something was really relevant to the report that we wrote as a group because we were making judgments about cause and effect." And she argues that's true even more broadly: "In government, all of our debates on tough policy choices really came down in my mind to some hypothesis, deduced, but not made explicit; . . . and once you pull it out of people, you force people to articulate their hypothesis. You can quickly make the point that it is actually a hypothesis and not a conclusion or a finding. And sometimes it is a hypothesis with significant or scarce evidence behind it."

There are a remarkable number of journalists with advanced degrees, including law degrees and medical degrees, many covering their "areas." The reporter and editor Carla Anne Robbins, who spent a good part of her career at the *Wall Street Journal* (where she shared in two Pulitzer Prizes) and the *New York Times,* didn't plan to become a journalist when she started studying for a PhD in political science at the University of California, Berkeley. The more work she did on international affairs, the more she realized she wanted to be out in the "real world" asking questions. (In 1985, three years after finishing her dissertation on Cuba, she got to interview Fidel Castro for a news story and tried to work in a few of the questions still left standing from her research.) She says, "at first, breaking into the news business with a PhD was hard; there was a faux anti-intellectualism." But after she proved she had the basic skills, her expertise was increasingly valued: "You don't need to get a PhD to be a disciplined thinker. But it made me a more critical thinker and an infinitely better researcher. I think it has made me a better editor and reporter."

Media outlets are a primary platform through which global events and policy debates are explained to the wider public. Many "beat" reporters who work on national security, military affairs, intelligence, and similar subjects develop deep expertise on the issues and institutions they cover, some of them through graduate study. Doctoral training can also help journalists evaluate and translate complex technical dimensions of government policy, as well as social science research, for public audiences.

Alexandra Evans got her PhD in history at the University of Virginia and went on to work at a nonprofit research organization: "I think the PhD provides a leg up for breaking down questions, for thinking about creative uses of data to get perfect answers, definitely for writing, and a familiarity with the literature that's not on that specific widget, being able to contextualize a problem, to very quickly do literature reviews, and to evaluate what is good and what is not. Because I already know the journals, I already know the names, I kind of can understand, even though it's not my field, where the centers of gravity are."

These abilities gained from a PhD are helpful even when the degree itself is not required for a particular job. Jon Rosenwasser received his PhD in international relations from the Fletcher School and serves on the Senate Select Committee on Intelligence as minority budget director, where he oversees the Office of the Director of National Intelligence. He reflects that his doctorate "is definitely not essential for the work I do now. But it gives me context for the oversight work I do so I can see issues in historical and political context and understand the dynamics that are driving the problems I work on. It also allows me to challenge how the government assesses problems and test the appropriateness of their policy response." He continues that being able to bring "methodological rigor to bear by credibly asking questions like, 'What are your assumptions? What data are you relying on? And what metrics are you using to evaluate success?' [That focus] stands people at attention."

Wesley Reisser also points out that diversity of academic discipline, like other forms of diversity, adds to the richness and quality of the policy process. In Reisser's case, "being the only geographer at the table" turned out to set him apart and was highly relevant for the issues he was working on at the State Department. "I'm in a room full of political scientists and economists," he continues, "because most of the State Department policy workers are from those two fields. And at the time, working on the Israeli-Palestinian conflict, when there were actually negotiations, having a geographer on the team who really could talk about borders and the status of Jerusalem and refugee issues with a much deeper academic background was a win-win for everybody."

Reuben Brigety also notes the value of doctoral training for high-level policy debates, in getting senior officials around the table focused on "questions that only they can answer." He notes, "There's often a tendency, even when you have very few people, for people to focus on the nitty-gritty, the nuts and bolts of how to approach this stuff that other people can do." Policymakers are not supposed to focus on simpler questions of implementation but on "giving guidance for the rest of government to focus on executing issues that they're supposed to execute." In his experience, the doctorate helped "formulate a question and really get down to the nub of what it is you're trying to get at, . . . to try and get to a particular solution."

What Should You Look For in a Doctoral Program?

If you are pretty confident you want to pursue an academic career, then getting a PhD from a top-ranked department in a particular discipline is probably the most important thing you can do. Departments in any field excel at socializing students into an academic career path, and they give students the tools they need (especially methodological approaches) to appeal to hiring committees later on.

If you aren't so confident you want to pursue an academic career, or you know you don't want to go into academia, then choosing a program gets a little trickier. Some disciplinary departments do have faculty with experience and/or favorable attitudes toward the policy world, but it pays to look carefully at your options.

It's worth looking closely at the faculty of any department or school to which you are considering applying. Rebecca Wolfe describes how fortunate she was to be the Harvard psychologist Herbert Kelman's last student in his long and distinguished career and how supportive he was of her ambitions in the policy world because of his own deep experience convening track-two negotiations on the Israeli-Palestinian conflict. But going to a graduate program to work with one particular person doesn't always work out. After all, what if the person retires before you are able to work with them, is not granted tenure, or leaves for another university? Some universities have policy-oriented centers or programs that may not themselves grant PhDs. But the faculties of those programs often have tremendous expertise advising students interested in nonacademic careers, so it is worth finding out if faculty affiliates can serve on dissertation committees.

An increasing number of policy schools offer PhDs in the fields of public policy and/or international affairs. The faculties of policy schools tend to come from a variety of disciplines—including political science, history, and economics—as well as fields such as sociology, geography, anthropology, psychology, and public health. For students who know they want to pursue a policy career upon entering graduate school, policy schools can provide a great option. There are faculty members at these schools with either experience in the policy world or at least a favorable predisposition to send students on to policy careers. It doesn't mean that every faculty member will be supportive, but you can gravitate toward those who are. As Alice Hunt Friend, who worked in the policy world before and during her doctoral program, noted of her experience getting a PhD at American University's School of International Service, "I found that there were two kinds of professors at AU. There were the professors who were friendly toward policy, and they were on a spectrum of really wanting to be involved in policy themselves, and they would occasionally ask me for advice. Or they were like, philosophically OK with it, but they didn't really get it. But at any rate, they were a safe space. And then there were the old-school professors who were really irritated with me for distracting myself in any way, shape, or form." Tanvi Madan chose her public policy program at the University of Texas at Austin over a history doctoral program because the policy school gave her the flexibility she was looking for—to include history faculty and historical methods but not to be wedded to all the discipline's norms regarding what was important.

One program that stood out in our research for its deliberate focus on preparing doctoral students for either academic or policy careers is the MIT Security Studies Program (SSP), which is focused particularly on issues surrounding the use of force and strategy. Sara Plana, a recent PhD from SSP, reflects, "I chose MIT, partly because MIT was one of the places that was the friendliest to people who were interested both in disseminating and engaging with policy communities and also open to having graduates go into policy careers. When I was looking at programs I always asked for that." Many years earlier, Ivo Daalder made the same decision. He studied with MIT professors like George Rathjens, Jack Ruina, and Bill Kaufman, who had all worked in government, on government councils, or at think tanks. "This idea of scientific approaches to policy problems was pretty much what MIT did, and it's why MIT was so different from Harvard, or even to some extent the Fletcher School."

A lesson for any program that wants to train graduate students for multiple career paths is to consider what all of them need regardless of their professional aspirations and then enable flexibility beyond that. In MIT's SSP, all students go through the same training until it's time to write their thesis. Barry Posen, director emeritus of SSP, told us, "They all study the same stuff, they all take the same courses." As for methods, he notes, "the difference between what's required and what's peer pressured is quite stark. So, students feel pressured to take more methods courses than what's actually required." But, says Posen, "the real parting of the ways probably comes when the thesis topic is generated." The students who want to go into academia or want that option do a deeper dive in methods and make sure to do a methods chapter in their dissertation. Students who aren't going on to academic careers don't need a dissertation that stresses theory and methods.

Key to any program that strives to support students with proclivities for policy careers is not to focus attention (and rewards) solely on the academic faculty members who place students in faculty positions at top-ranked universities but rather to celebrate those members who enable students to pursue their interests, wherever those take them within academia or outside it. And they should, like MIT's SSP, celebrate students who go on to make an impact in policy careers.

It's a common situation for students to feel like they are "letting down" their PhD committees if they decide to pursue a policy career. Some of that is going to come from the students regardless, but faculty should not exacerbate it. William Ruger, despite his successes outside academia, says, "If you leave, there is going to be something that nags at you. You need to be self-aware, when you do this [i.e., go the nonacademic route], that it's going to nag, particularly if you're making a decision like I did to leave a tenured job." He is grateful to his faculty mentor, Brandeis professor Robert Art, who, says Ruger, "wasn't the kind of guy that thought unless you become an academic and look just like me, that can't be a good career." Similarly, Robert Kahn feels fortunate that his PhD supervisor at MIT was Paul Krugman, who was respected in both the academic and policy communities. "Paul, to his credit," says Kahn, "was very open and supportive of any choice that I was going to make, . . . whatever it was that gave me passion."

Methods Will Help You in Any Career, but Other Skills Are Important as Well

Another theme that emerged from our interviews is that more training in research methods serves policy workers well. Posen argues, "The quantitative facility is a real asset to get for wargaming, for modeling and simulation, for consuming budget data. I've noticed that the students are very facile with modeling very quickly. So, those political science methods courses pay off in a totally different way for us, and for them, because if they walk into the door at the RAND Corporation, or a place like that, that's doing modeling and simulation, those people can kind of get up to speed really quick."

Those going into the policy world don't necessarily have to produce a dissertation that's heavy on research methods, particularly quantitative research methods, but they need to be sufficiently versed in quantitative methods to be able to evaluate claims made based on them. Tanvi Madan recalls that her mentor, James Steinberg, who served in high-level positions in the Clinton and Obama administrations, told her that her ability to understand statistics would prove important for what she wanted to do: "His point was . . . you will someday have somebody come to you with a report and say 'This is what I found.' You should be able to evaluate it and . . . ask questions about the research design." Mara Revkin concurs: "I do regret that I didn't invest more time in coding and quantitative methods training, which didn't come as easily to me as qualitative methods. It's important to be proficient in a range of methods, even methods you don't plan to use, just to be able to critically evaluate other research in your field." When he was in graduate school, Morgan Kaplan took a causal inference course that he loved, and the next course in the sequence was a quantitative methods course that his professors encouraged him to take. "I opted not to," he says, "and I still regret that. I regret it because I do think that, beyond academia, having a stronger quantitative skill set would have been helpful. I took it upon myself to build that out later, especially as I became an editor [at *International Security*]."

It may seem obvious that a deep understanding of quantitative research methods will serve economics PhDs well as they go on to different types of careers. But even in that field, there are choices students can make that will boost their appeal with prospective employers. Erik Durbin, after completing his economics PhD at Columbia, went into a tenure-track position at the Olin School of Business at Washington University in Saint Louis before pursuing a policy career; he has held government jobs at the Federal Trade Commission, the Council of Economic Advisers, and the Consumer Financial Protection Bureau. He says that his message to students who want to pursue an economics career in policy is to focus "on empirical skills. This may be true in academia today as well, but certainly within the government jobs and consulting as well, it's applied data skills that are really kind of the day-to-day tool that people are looking for. And so, that would be one thing [to focus on in school]: less on theory and more on applied data work."

It's not just government where these methods skills are important. There's also the NGO world. Dafna Rand recalls of her work at Mercy Corps, "Being forced to take some degree of quantitative reasoning . . . has been really helpful to be able to enable and work with a whole group of people focusing on quantitative impact evaluations. I built up the research team at Mercy Corps hiring these types of quantitative experts. I didn't know or remember the specific method that they were using but I knew enough to know that their approaches were trying to use sophisticated methods to evaluate impact of State and USAID programs in greater depth and scope."

Of course, spending time and course credits in graduate school on quantitative methods comes with trade-offs. If you are taking methods, you might not be developing regional or language expertise. If you are focusing just on research, you may not be getting teaching experience. The key is to be aware of your choices and to seek to allocate your coursework and other grad school opportunities in ways that reflect your own interests and ambitions, not what other students or even faculty say you "should" do. Mara Revkin recalls, "I remember a faculty member saying in a professional development meeting for PhD students that our goal should be to spend as close to 100 percent of your time on research as possible and to try to minimize teaching and service." You may have heard something similar in your PhD program. It's worth noting that such advice may be unhelpful, as much for those seeking teaching jobs as for those who are developing skills for a policy environment, where teamwork, personnel management, and briefing skills are in demand.

Getting teaching experience in graduate school isn't just helpful for you if you want a teaching career. Teaching provides doctoral students with opportunities to learn how to boil down complex material to convey key points to an audience, a skill that is important across domains. Jennifer McArdle launched herself on a successful start-up career while finishing her degree at King's College London, and she previously taught at Salve Regina University. "Being a professor or teaching," she says, "helps when working in defense with the government because it inevitably gives you a level of credibility. Obviously, you're well-spoken, you can take complex topics and make them accessible to a more general audience. The moment you say, 'I used to teach graduate or undergraduate students,' people respond positively as they assume you possess some form of subject matter expertise. I think PhD candidates should aspire, if they can, to get some teaching experience, as it will pay dividends later—even in industry."

Jon Rosenwasser notes that, indeed, many graduate school skills have application in the policy world: "Research skills are always helpful—the ability to know what questions to ask, where to find reliable information (and debunk bad or misinformation), how to conduct rigorous analysis using multiple kinds of qualitative and quantitative methods, and how to synthesize and present arguments (and anticipate and defend against counterarguments) in both written and oral formats. Above all, students need to demonstrate that they care about and are interested in solving real-world problems, not just admiring them from a remote academic perch." But he adds, "Employers will know PhD students have expertise in a couple of topics and broad knowledge in a field. But they want to know if students have a conceptual agility that can travel to other policy issue areas. Additionally, employers want to know the students are not just ivory tower brainiacs, but know how to organize a team, define tasks, and execute— that is, get things done, not just think big thoughts." Experience as a teaching assistant, discussion section leader, or student committee representative can help with demonstrating those skills, as we discuss below when we turn to creating a résumé that appeals to prospective employers.

Revkin also highlights a key point: whatever you choose to focus your time on in graduate school, use it well. "Mastering any skill or subject has startup costs. I spent a lot of time learning and maintaining Arabic language skills and developing research partnerships with organizations, which was time that I didn't spend taking all the advanced statistics classes. I could have learned more methods and learned them better if I had not invested so much time in field research and area specialization, but I think my work would have been less interesting, so it's a trade-off."

Morgan Kaplan also took Arabic and studied the Middle East as an undergraduate at George Washington University, but his first real research trip to the region came during the summer between his second and third years of graduate school in Jordan. He received a Foreign Language and Area Studies fellowship from the Department of Education to enhance his Arabic language skills. After studying in Jordan, he went on to do research that summer in the West Bank with funding from a separate grant. He reflects that graduate programs should help students better prepare to do fieldwork. Eliminating the culture of "'figure it out when you get there' would help students be prepared to meet the intellectual and emotional challenges of fieldwork. There's a lot of the anxiety and stress that graduate students go through when they go into the field." It can also be dangerous, as he admits was the case when he went to Iraq in the summer of 2014.

Individuals who come out of graduate school with expertise in another culture or region will be greatly valued in certain parts of the policy community—for example, regional offices in agencies like US-AID, the Department of State, and the Department of Defense; think tank centers; and regionally focused committees on Capitol Hill. Note that a number of area experts with PhDs joined the Biden administration, including Ely Ratner (China) and Celeste Wallander (Russia) at the Department of Defense, Dafna Rand (Middle East) at the State Department, and Rush Doshi (China) and Amanda Sloat (Europe) at the National Security Council. (Similarly, there are PhDs with functional expertise at senior levels of the Biden administration, such as the defense expert Kathleen Hicks, the deputy secretary of defense, and Bonnie Jenkins, the undersecretary of state for arms control and international security affairs, who is an expert on weapons of mass destruction, nonproliferation, and arms control.) Building this expertise takes time. Some of this knowledge can come from courses or from study abroad or from overseas fieldwork. But, as Revkin points out, the time spent developing that expertise is time not spent on other pursuits, such as more methods training. There is no one-size-fits-all answer to where you should focus your attention in your graduate school training.

The most important takeaway for students who don't want their time in graduate school to stretch out endlessly is simply to be aware of the trade-offs you are making. Most of the people we spoke with did cite their methods training as incredibly important for the careers they pursued. But there are other valuable skills that one can develop in school. As we have just seen, having area and language expertise, including time living abroad in the field, can be extremely valuable. And building success in the private sector might mean pursuing opportunities to build skills outside your graduate program. McArdle, for example, notes, "My PhD [was] partially funded by the modeling and simulation community in Orlando. I was able to facilitate that by first publishing in well-read defense policy outlets on synthetic training, something that the defense industry community deeply cares about. I also worked to develop technical expertise. I've become certified in modeling and simulation, and I have worked closely with software engineers and applied scientists to really understand the tools and technologies that are core components of synthetic environments." Similarly, Paul McLachlan, who moved from a staff position at Emory University to Silicon Valley, says that in his world, there are now a large number of "boot camps or programs that are specialized in taking a PhD and getting them to scale within four or five months. These programs can be really effective and can help people learn skills they did not acquire in graduate school"—for example, in coding.

Finding Your Tribe

The Bridging the Gap initiative has been hosting an annual PhD New Era workshop since 2006. Bringing together about twenty to twenty-five students (mostly, but not exclusively, from political science, history, and international relations programs) from around the country and overseas, the two-and-a-half-day program uses comparative scenario analysis to help generate policy-relevant research questions.[4]

When students first started coming to the New Era workshop in the mid-2000s, they felt relieved to be able to discuss their interests in policy-relevant research and even policy careers in a safe space. They reported how nervous they were back in their home departments about discussing these issues with their faculty advisers. They were grateful to have found a group of people who had similar goals and with whom they could build a network. As Tanvi Madan reflects, "I did these workshops that would kind of make you feel that you weren't alone in this world as a crazy person who was doing a PhD but also interested in policy. You discover that your tribe is bigger than you think. And that ends up being your network."

The historian James Graham Wilson did archival research seminars in Washington that helped him connect with scholars like the National Security Archive's Svetlana Savranskaya, who enabled him to get access to materials at the Gorbachev Foundation that helped him develop as the type of scholar who was then able to land a job at the State Department Historian's Office. Jon Rosenwasser became a term member at the Council on Foreign Relations, and Alice Hunt Friend developed affiliations with the Center for a New American Security and the Center for Strategic and International Studies.

Building these networks is crucial. Today, there's much less feeling among PhD students attending New Era and similar programs that they have to hide their interests when they are in their PhD programs. One reason is the tremendous growth in the number of programs catering to these interests. Another is the fact that enough alumni of these programs have over time moved into faculty positions at a range of colleges and universities across the United States that enable them to encourage a more diverse next generation to pursue these opportunities. But just as building networks is important in academia—for learning about conferences and workshops, for being considered for postdocs and tenure-track faculty positions, for other types of grants and fellowships—so too is it important in the policy world. The old adage that "it's not what you know, it's who you know," isn't quite right, since, after all, it's both, but it gets at an important point: finding and building networks is critical to career development.

Is all lost if you don't attend one of these programs? No. Another way to build your networks is to cold call or cold email people in the policy world whose work you admire or whose job is one you think might be a good fit for you. You can write them and say you'd like to hear more about their work and tell them a bit about yours. It might sound scary, but most people who have succeeded in the policy world were once in your shoes and cold emailed (or faxed, if they're older). You'd be surprised how willing people are to help. You don't want to be a pest, so if they don't respond after one or two attempts, you can move on. If they don't respond, you are no worse off than you were before you reached out. And if you don't reach them, you can always cold email us!

One way to meet some of these people beyond the short-term programs is by joining networking organizations, attending workshops or conferences where you might even be able to present your work, or pursuing internships. We discuss a number of these opportunities below, and more extensive lists can be found in the appendixes.

Membership Organizations

A plethora of programs have developed that are focused on helping underrepresented groups make connections in order to overcome the "old boys network," particularly in fields like national security that have been dominated by white men in the past. Graduate school is a great time to look at joining some of these groups because they can provide peers and mentors who can answer your questions and direct you to other opportunities. In the national security and international affairs fields, there are long-standing networks like Women in International Security, which has built a global network since its founding in 1987, and Black Professionals in International Affairs, which was founded in 1989. There are also relatively newer endeavors—such as Women of Color Advancing Peace, Security, and Conflict Transformation, #NatSecGirlSquad, and Out in National Security for LGBTQIA-identifying people—which have rapidly helped numerous individuals create networks in recent years. The Leadership Council for Women in National Security developed to help elevate women to senior-level US government positions, and there are a number of networks like Young Professionals in Foreign Policy and the Foreign Policy for America Next Generation initiative that are helping individuals at earlier points in their careers make the connections they need to pursue entry-level positions or move up the ladder. There are also next-generation foreign policy efforts focused on cultivating politically liberal cohorts (e.g., the Truman National Security Project) and politically conservative cohorts (the John Quincy Adams Society). Some of these organizations have conferences you can attend in person or virtually, and many have job boards.

Workshops and Programs

In addition to these kinds of membership programs helping to build networks in the national security field and beyond, there are a number of workshops, summer programs, and pre- and postdoc opportunities that enable policy-interested students to meet like-minded colleagues with whom they can learn. In the national security arena, the Summer Workshop on the Analysis of Military Operations and Strategy has been held for more than twenty-five years. It is designed, its organizers state, "to expose young scholars to a body of knowledge that is seldom made available in conventional graduate programs; to encourage some of them to specialize in the field; to nurture a critical mass of academics competent to contribute to defense policy debates; to preserve expertise in strategic studies outside of government; and to foster a network of analysts committed to supporting each other and promoting the field within academia."[5]

Many of the programs that have developed since the mid-2000s are funded by the Carnegie Corporation of New York, which has aggressively sought to build networks of PhD students and faculty who want to pursue policy-relevant research. These include the Bridging the Gap New Era workshop, which in addition to its scenario exercises includes professional development sessions; the International Policy Scholars Consortium and Network (IPSCON), which "aims to create a cohort of scholar-practitioners who understand the problems and perspectives of each world and can successfully pursue careers in both"; and the Clements Center for National Security Summer Seminar in History and Statecraft, where "participants explore the relationship between historical insights and national security policymaking."[6]

These programs can help early career scholars branch out beyond their disciplinary focus. Alexandra Evans found IPSCON helpful "because I met nonhistorians, and I could see what fellowships and grants they'd applied to and what activities they were part of. And it opened up my eyes to this whole other world of conferences. There's not just the International Studies Association and the Society for Historians of American Foreign Relations and the American Political Science Association, there are all these smaller workshops that aren't advertised as publicly and may be more interdisciplinary." Evans attended IPSCON, Bridging the Gap, and the Clements Center Summer Seminar and held an Ernest May Fellowship at the Belfer Center at Harvard.

Sara Plana notes, "I would absolutely recommend all the professional development workshops; they are not mutually exclusive. You can do them all and they all do different things and they all help you with different things and I think that is such a strength. I did two of the main ones, IPSCON and Bridging the Gap, and they are very different and gave me different networks, different skills, and different ways of bridging the gap. . . . I think the main [value of the workshops] to me was actually finding a network of scholars and mentors who were committed to scholarship and also practice."

Some are not very time consuming (and they tend to cover the travel and lodging costs for participants), such as Bridging the Gap's

New Era Workshop, the Johns Hopkins School of Advanced International Studies' Kissinger Center's International Policy Scholars Consortium and Network, the Summer Workshop on the Analysis of Military Operations and Strategy, and the Clements Center Summer Seminar on History and Statecraft. (A more complete listing of these programs, including many outside the national security area, can be found in appendix A.) The New Era workshop, for example, is only two and a half days, and the Clements Center program is less than a week (which is too bad, because it is located in Beaver Creek, Colorado). The time involved may be less noticeable to your advisers than what it tells them about your interests, but an increasing number of faculty at top-ranked doctoral programs are viewing these kinds of opportunities as useful for their students' network and skill development, and they are eager for their students to participate in them. These workshops will help you better understand policy opportunities and will help you create networks, especially with other like-minded students. In fact, you may find that if you go to one of these, you will also see your new friends at the next workshop.

Mary Barton recalls, "From the beginning, I was pretty open to working in the government and trying to come to DC, but it took a lot of work and effort to get a job here and from early on, and that's my sense from other people's experiences too." She also pursued Bridging the Gap, IPSCON, and the Clements Center seminar, where she had the opportunity "to meet people who worked in DC and learn about what it entailed. So, I wanted that, I wanted to go for that, and I was lucky to have mentors who supported that ambition."

Other endeavors are more intensive, such as summer internships and the kinds of engineering bootcamps and programs that are valuable for getting hired in Silicon Valley, or the type of wargaming and simulation certificates that Jennifer McArdle pursued, giving her the skills she needed to go join a start-up (and that were helpful when she was teaching at a university).

Summer Programs and Internships

The RAND Corporation, the Center for Naval Analyses, and the Institute for Defense Analyses are federally funded research-and-development centers that offer paid summer experiences in the policy world that may also help in getting a security clearance. These opportunities can be great chances to learn about policy work and might even lead to future employment.

The economist Erik Durbin, who works at a domestic policy agency but whose insights are relevant for those interested in foreign policy, says that those students who want to pursue policy careers should look at spending a summer interning at a government agency or think tank to build connections. He notes that this also has value: "If you're on the fence as to whether you really want to pursue academia or go to a policy job, then it could really help to learn more about what an economist's life is like outside academia." In economics, hiring for both academic and nonacademic jobs takes place at the discipline's annual meeting. He says, "Often when we're deciding who to interview, who to fly out, all that kind of stuff, one of the main considerations is, Is this person getable? Is this somebody who would take an offer if we made them one? In that conversation, some strong signal that 'I want to be in Washington, DC, I'm not interested in academic work, I'm very interested in policy work,' that can play a big role." Demonstrating those interests in graduate school can be quite valuable for landing a government economics position.

There are opportunities (some paid) available across government that students can take advantage of during a graduate school summer. Sara Plana did an internship at the Office of the Secretary of Defense between her first and second years in her PhD program. Others in her class were doing research for their second-year paper or working as a research assistant for a professor. Plana had previously worked at the Department of Defense, but not in policy, and she wanted to see what working in a policy office was like to see if she thought it might be something she would want to do in the future. She notes, "If you're interested in exploring a particular part of the US government, or think tank, there are opportunities to get temporarily employed as an intern, or you can be a nonresident fellow for some think tanks and get the opportunity to understand how that works. I only did it [the Defense internship] for two months, and I learned so much about how the sausage gets made." Similarly, Dafna Rand spent the summer after her first year at Columbia on an internship at the State Department's

Near Eastern Affairs Bureau. Her experience solidified her interests in policy work, and she points out that "those work relationships have stayed with me forever." When she was writing her dissertation, she also spent twelve months in multiple countries in the Middle East on a Boren Fellowship, and she says that kind of experience is invaluable in policy: "If you want to work at State or USAID, it's just a calling card. Have you spent time deeply understanding a culture anywhere in the world? Do you speak a foreign language? Have you done work in a foreign language abroad? Just to get along with your colleagues, to understand diplomats' perspective on their mission, these types of field experiences are invaluable."

Boren Fellowships provide deep immersion in foreign languages and culture and are taken during graduate school; in fact, the awardees have to remain in their program for the duration of the fellowship. The minimum time spent on the program is twelve weeks, but applicants are strongly encouraged to spend twenty-five weeks for continuous study overseas. While the focus for graduate students is on greater language proficiency, awardees are encouraged to do research for their dissertations. At the graduate level, there is a summer domestic program option to help students gain enough proficiency before spending time overseas acquiring more advanced language skills. For students who want to gain area expertise—which can be of particular interest for congressional committees, the State Department, and the intelligence community—a Boren Fellowship can prove hugely beneficial, as was the case for Dafna Rand. The Boren program includes a service obligation that creates opportunities to secure a permanent position in the US government, particularly since those administering the Boren Scholarships and Fellowships program provide resources toward finding federal employment.[7]

Beyond seminars and summer experiences, there are a growing number of predoctoral and postdoctoral fellowships geared toward helping students develop their interests in producing policy-relevant research. As appendix A indicates, these include programs at universities, think tanks, and professional military schools. Durbin reports that the Consumer Financial Protection Bureau, where he works, has in the past offered longer-term internships that serve as predoctoral fellowships that give people an opportunity to do research for their degree but also get exposed to the kind of policy work his agency does. There may also be opportunities for you to work as a consultant. Mara Revkin points to short-term consulting opportunities with UN agencies, since those are typically no more than three months and could be done over a summer. In her case, some did run longer, and she "studied for some exams from Egypt and submitted my dissertation from Iraq." But she found the work invaluable. Those consulting gigs often arise, as Revkin's initially did, from writing an article in a publication designed for broader public and policy audiences. If you write something that grabs someone's attention in the policy world, they may reach out to engage you directly.

We can't avoid the fact that these experiences—seminars, workshops, and summer internships in expensive cities—are not easily available to all doctoral students. Although these types of programs are typically funded, with participant expenses covered, it still may be difficult for you to take time off to do them if you are working full time to put yourself through school or if you have to arrange or rearrange childcare. Even a paid internship in Washington is unlikely to match the earning potential of other summer jobs or cover the high expense of rent in a major East Coast city.

Increasingly, policy schools and graduate departments are under pressure to provide funding to support students in exploiting these types of opportunities. DC-based organizations are likewise under pressure to pay summer interns a living wage—although a paid internship in the executive branch was rare until 2022, when the State Department and then the White House announced new paid internship programs. As the national security sector heightens its long-overdue focus on equity and inclusion, we hope that these various opportunities will become more financially accessible to more doctoral students—and we urge you, if you see a program you think will benefit you, to *ask* both the program sponsor and your department/school how they can make it possible for you to participate. But we want to assure you that while these experiences are beneficial, they are not essential. Kristin Lord, CEO of the education and development nonprofit IREX, lacked both the resources and the advice to even be aware of such opportunities. She notes, "I didn't have any networks and I didn't have any money. And I did OK."

Do What You Love

If there's one piece of advice that comes up over and over in talking with policy people who received their PhD in a social science discipline, it's that you should write your dissertation on a topic you are passionate about. Don't try to guess what will be popular when you are finished, because what's fashionable changes. The interest in PhDs with expertise on pandemics or race, for example, changed dramatically between 2019 and 2021. As Sara Plana reports, "I was truly fortunate to have a dissertation topic that just motivated me throughout, . . . and that propelled me forward throughout graduate school. . . . It's important in many respects for me, and I've convinced myself it is important for the world." Reuben Brigety advises, "Passion beats discipline every day of the week; . . . you focus on where your passion is, and you get really good at it so that the world has to come to you because they need somebody who's really good at that."

Also choose your dissertation committee carefully. Find a topic you love but also find a committee whose members are open to your interests in policy. Carla Anne Robbins reflects, "I studied political science because I was interested in politics. And when I got to graduate school, I discovered for a lot of people, it wasn't that. But I gravitated toward professors for whom it was." Tanvi Madan says, "I know of others who had several problems with their committees because they had different goals in mind. . . . Everybody on my committee, even if they didn't have policy experience, was comfortable engaging with the policy world, and that made a huge difference." Kori Schake cites her mentors—Condoleezza Rice, Catherine Kelleher, and Thomas Schelling—as the key to pursuing and finishing her degree and going on to the career she has had. "[Schelling] forced me through all my graduate coursework in a year while taking both sets of comprehensive exams, while working on my prospectus. Because Tom always thought I was a flight risk, and forcing me through to what was going to be interesting, what I actually wanted to do the work on, was how Tom conceptualized doing his job. . . . I would not be in this profession if my mentors had tried to channel me into a tenure track academic education. . . . They saw my strengths and weaknesses and consciously pushed me toward work they could see my eyes lit up in the doing of it."

And as you go through graduate school, keep in mind Jon Rosenwasser's words of wisdom: "The best dissertation is a done dissertation." If you are lucky, you'll find yourself in Wesley Reisser's situation: "The most important thing is that you get the degree and you finish the degree and find a way to do it that you will enjoy and that isn't painful. I had fun both researching and writing my dissertation, it was fascinating. And because I had fun, it also went by quickly." Those truly are words to live by for any PhD student.

Notes

1. Daniel W. Drezner, "So You Want to Get a Ph.D. to Get Ahead in DC," *Foreign Policy*, November 29, 2012, https://foreignpolicy.com/2012/11/29/so-you-want-to-get-a-ph-d-to-get-ahead-in-dc/.

2. As the George Washington University professor Melani McAlister bluntly puts it, "Your undying passion for the material has to sustain you through somewhere between 5 and 8 difficult years in which you make little money and therefore make no contributions to your retirement, save no money for vacations, and live with high levels of stress, with absolutely no guarantee of employment in your field after you finish." See her PhD advice at https://melanimcalister.com/thinking-twice-about-grad-school/.

3. See Research on International Policy Implementation Lab (RIPIL), https://bridgingthegapproject.org/ripil/.

4. For a discussion of the uses of scenario analysis based on lessons learned from these workshops, see Naazneen H. Barma, Brent Durbin, Eric Lorber, and Rachel E. Whitlark, "'Imagine a World in Which': Using Scenarios in Political Science," *International Studies Perspectives* 17, no. 2 (May 2016): 117–35.

5. Summer Workshop on the Analysis of Military Operations and Strategy (SWAMOS), https://www.siwps.org/programs/summer-workshop-on-the-analysis-of-military-operations-and-strategy/.

6. More information about these programs is available at https://bridgingthegapproject.org/programs/new-era/; https://sais.jhu.edu/kissinger/ipscon; and https://www.clementscenter.org/press/item/2035-summer-seminar-in-history-and-statecraft-2021-applications-now-open.

7. On eligibility, see https://www.borenawards.org/eligible-programs#basic. On the National Security Education Program (NSEP) service requirement, which includes the Boren Fellows and Scholars, see https://www.borenawards.org/sites/default/files/service_requirement_sheet_317.pdf. We are grateful to Andrew Radin for highlighting these programs.

3

Envisioning Yourself in Policy Work

Graduate students drawn to applied work are often told that it's easy to move from academia to policy work but very difficult to go in the other direction, because if you've been away from academia for a while, you likely won't be engaged in the kind of publishing that will allow you to get hired in a faculty position. Therefore, many advisers and mentors will tell you that it's best to finish your doctorate, find an academic job, get published, and get tenure before pursuing your interest in policy. Once you have job security, you can afford to turn your attention to intellectual pursuits that have traditionally been less valued by academia and to take breaks from your academic work for programs like the Council on Foreign Relations' International Affairs Fellowship and the American Political Science Association's Congressional Fellowship, take a political appointment in government, or pursue other temporary arrangements in policy positions for which you might be granted a leave by your home university. Senior academics will warn you that if you take a policy job right after finishing your PhD, it will be difficult if not impossible to go back to a university-based position later on.

This advice can make a lot of sense if you really want an academic career. But our engagement with more than two dozen policy-focused PhDs makes clear that this approach is far too restrictive (even setting aside the challenge of finding a tenure-track position if you want one). There are as many ways to combine academic and policy work over the course of a career as there are individuals doing so. Many career public servants, like the State Department's Wesley Reisser, teach as adjunct professors at Washington-area universities; Reisser even serves on the Council of the American Geographical Society and is considering a full-time teaching career after he retires from the US Civil Service. Some full-time government employees continue to attend academic conferences, collaborate with academic colleagues, and publish academic work while serving in policy roles (although their writing is often subject to prepublication reviews). Others maintain an active hand in academic endeavors from a think tank perch, where they can mentor pre- and postdoctoral scholars; where they publish for general audiences, policy audiences, and academic audiences alike; and where they remain connected to academic colleagues and attend conferences, which also help them recruit rising talent for their organizations and identify promising new research with applications to their policy areas. It's also possible to spend a career outside academia and then take up a university position down the road, as Carla Anne Robbins and Rebecca Wolfe have done. You will hear more about these career trajectories in chapter 6.

It's also important to note that even if you have a career as a professor, you can pursue policy interests in myriad ways from academia. You can write for broader audiences—in policy journals and magazines, op-eds, and blog posts, as well as being on podcasts, to which anyone with a commute might be listening. Recent surveys conducted by the Teaching, Research, and International Policy program at William & Mary show that, particularly in the trade and development fields, policymakers are utilizing academic work.[1] You can also serve in policy roles yourself, as many scholars have done, taking a year or two of leave from their home institutions to work in government or at an international organization.

Many of the individuals with whom we spoke for this book described being drawn both to academic pursuits like training students and deep research and to the direct impact of policy work. No matter what your career plans are now, it's worth asking yourself what it is about academia that you most enjoy or most value: Is it teaching? Writing? Mentoring young people? Research and investigation? Data analysis? That's because while there are many ways to combine academic and policy work over the course of one's career, it is also possible to find ways to "scratch the itch" of what you love to do in academia from within a policy career. For example, one book on finding your path outside academia wisely notes that "an enormous variety of PhDs tell us that their new careers—as policy wonks, management consultants, public relations executives, and computer gurus—involve some form of teaching. Just because you're not turning in grades at the end of the semester doesn't mean that you're not using your ability to mentor, instruct, and inspire."[2]

Frequently, when we are approached by PhDs seeking to move into foreign policy work, they ask about two specific workplaces: "government" and think tanks. This may be because PhDs are looking for places in the policy sphere where they can do what they have been trained to do: analyze. But even within government and think tanks, not all the jobs available are primarily analytical, and the universe of policy careers is far broader and more diverse than these two sectors.

This chapter seeks to help you think through how to match your own personality, preferences, and ambitions with different types of applied policy environments. In the next chapter, we then provide an overview of the wide array of employment sectors within what we call the "foreign policy ecosystem."

How Do You Like to Work?

In considering whether foreign policy work is right for you, and what types of policy work and work environments might suit you best, we suggest asking yourself four key questions:

- Where do I fit along the continuum from "thinker" to "doer"?
- How do I like to engage the problems I'm trying to address: from close up or far away?
- Do I prefer to work on my own or as part of a team?
- Am I more motivated by answering a question / solving a puzzle or by working to fulfill a vision or mission?

In our conversations with PhD policy professionals, we found that these four questions are among the aspects of their working environments that have mattered most to their fulfillment and happiness in their careers. Take note: there is no "right" or "wrong" answer to these questions for policy-minded PhDs. All the possible directions for each question discussed below point to exciting opportunities in the policy sphere. But understanding your own work style and preferences can help guide you to the kinds of applied work that you will probably enjoy most.

There is great general advice available in a variety of formats for taking your PhD into a nonacademic career, such as taking a personality or interests inventory or making lists of what you love and hate about academic work and using that to guide your job search.[3] We encourage you to explore personality inventories, guidebooks, and other tools. There are also career coaches and workshops targeted to those transitioning out of academic careers.

Although the range of policy careers is wide, policy jobs all share one focus: *solving people's problems*. When government is working at its best, this is what it does. And a host of organizations partner with governments, or press governments, or persuade governments on which problems demand policy attention and what to do to solve them. The four questions we propose to help guide you in considering policy careers, therefore, are focused on how you think about people, problems, and solutions. Let's examine each question in detail.

Where Do I Fit along the Continuum from "Thinker" to "Doer"?

Getting a PhD in the social sciences means undertaking deep research to understand a complex phenomenon, answer a hard question, and/ or analyze a challenging problem. We do not advise anyone to pursue a PhD if they don't enjoy the experience of deep research and have an intellectual area that fascinates them enough to drive them through the process of researching and writing a dissertation.

That said, some people rejoice at a vision for the rest of their career that closely resembles that dissertation-writing experience, and some do not. If your dissertation process was your ideal version of a working life but your intellectual interests tend more toward applied questions than theory building, or if other life preferences drive you away from academia, you might consider a role in the policy world that focuses on analysis and understanding, such as an intelligence analyst, think tank scholar, or a policy analyst for the Congressional Research Service. You might conduct research for an NGO concerned to improve policy in a given area. You might analyze and learn from the results of policy interventions—for example, by monitoring and evaluating projects for USAID or one of its contractors and grantees.

As in academia, policy analysis can go beyond case-specific work to examine how problems of a certain type can be solved through a common set of approaches or to understand how our collective experience in a certain case can illuminate new possibilities for policy toward similar cases in the future. When she served as vice president of policy and research at Mercy Corps, Dafna Rand says her job "was to bring in people and build up a team based on the idea that the integration of policy and research could enhance our impact as an organization and sector. Our Board of Advisers hired me in particular because they wanted us not only to say, this particular set of programs is reducing X or Y sources of violence and fragility in Niger but [also to say] that means that there's a sequence to how you would want to go help the Nigeriens, whether with diplomatic or programmatic interventions."

You may not be motivated as much by understanding a problem as by working to resolve it or at least improve it. If you like to put your knowledge directly into practice, if you are happiest when you can see the results of your work more immediately in the world, and/or if you like to tackle what's in front of you with creativity and persistence, trying to leave it better than you found it, then look for "doer" roles that go beyond analysis to policy formulation, advocacy, or execution, whether from a headquarters or out in the field.

If you are more of a "doer," that doesn't mean that your doctoral-level analytical skills are not relevant for your work. After all, many doers also need to spend time thinking. Often, jobs in policy demand both analysis and execution, and indeed the policy professionals you'll hear from throughout this book consistently cite their doctoral training in critical thinking and methods of analysis as something that sets them apart in debating, determining, and executing policies.

How Do I Like to Engage the Problems I'm Trying to Address: From Close Up or Far Away?

Looking at international affairs from the perspective of a doctoral student or a PhD, it's hard to imagine working through a problem without knowing a lot of context: What's the history of this problem? Who are the key players, and who has a stake in the outcome? What do we know about the way actors tend to behave in circumstances like this? What similar problems have we seen elsewhere, and how do those experiences inform the options for addressing this one? Of course, doctoral training puts an emphasis on using theory, along with various types of contextual data and careful research design, to increase the rigor and reliability of our understanding. And, as discussed above, the policy world often demands that we address problems with insufficient information and under time pressure, both of which limit analytical rigor. Even given these constraints, however, there are within the policy world options for working on problems with more time and distance and with more context, and there are options that are more on the fly and in the trenches. Your doctoral training can offer you advantages no matter which you prefer, but determining your preferences can help shape your professional trajectory.

Some of us are motivated by the idea of diving into the unfamiliar: by situations where we must quickly read the environment, size up the problem, and construct a solution that's fit to purpose—engaging directly with the people living with the problem (and who are often part of creating it!) and sometimes jerry-rigging solutions that may fit only that specific context or may last only for a certain period. If this describes you, then you may be happy working as a frontline diplomat, development worker, democracy builder, or civil society activist. If you can see yourself negotiating market entry to a country for a business, brokering a local cease-fire, or arranging the entry of urgent humanitarian aid into a disaster zone, then the "expeditionary" career path is an option to explore. You might thrive as a chief of party for a humanitarian group helping a community improve local health care or for an international NGO training and supporting local activists. You might build a career as a diplomat in the US Foreign Service, moving every two to four years to a new country (and occasionally back to Washington), where you learn to navigate new environments and cultures. You might also find joy in the private sector, helping an American company understand, enter, and navigate a new market in a country you know well or putting your background to work in management, something that is also extremely valuable in the NGO world.

Kristin Lord loved her doctoral program at Georgetown University, and she planned to be a professor, until the need for extra income led her to take a job running events and education programs. She relates, "I went into an office every day, I got things done, I was with other people, the timelines weren't two, three, four, or five years to accomplish something, they were much faster. I was good at it. It required a lot of project management and some creativity and some curriculum development and a lot of working with teams and so on. And I really love that. And so, I took that as evidence that I needed not be a professor. I was not hard-wired from a personality standpoint. I loved the research, I liked the teaching because I had taught a class at Georgetown. I really enjoyed all that, but I wasn't wired to go sit in the library by myself, and work on books that may not be done or published for years."

Do I Prefer to Work on My Own or as Part of a Team?

That PhDs are introverts is a common assumption, but of course it's not always true; and even introverts don't always enjoy working alone.

One of us has spent his career centered in academia and one has spent hers based in think tanks—but both of us coauthor frequently and joyfully, including the book you're holding in your hands. As academic social science refines its appreciation of quantitative research studies and the increase in computer-assisted analysis encourages scholars to build and make use of large data sets, we expect social science disciplines to gain even more appreciation of team-built, multiauthor research. And yet, in academia, success (whether defined as impact on the field or as career advancement) mostly derives from "getting credit" for one's individual contribution to the generation and/or application of knowledge.

On the whole, solo work is far less common in the policy sphere than in academia. Indeed, much policy work demands that teams of people operate less like members of a research lab and much more like a military unit or an orchestra: Each individual contributes specific functionality to the whole, submerging their individual ego in the common project. To succeed at the task, the group's members must clearly understand their shared goal and each individual's contribution to the work (including the relevant lines of authority and hierarchy that structure the group's work). This is particularly true in government, where there's generally even more anonymity in policy work than in an orchestra. You aren't listed in the program, and you likely won't be getting public credit for your work. Maybe you will be named in a subsequent academic study, or a memo you wrote will appear in a volume in the State Department's *Foreign Relations of the United States* series decades later. But in general, few people outside government will know you deserve credit for your contribution to a major arms control agreement or a new effort to combat climate change.

In graduate school, especially once we begin to undertake our own research, we are often encouraged to work alone, and we are told that coauthorship and collaboration reduce our unique value in the academic marketplace. "Getting credit" is very rarely an important component of policy impact, though it can play a role in professional advancement. Dafna Rand notes this difference between her graduate school experience and her work in the policy world: "You're taught that you need to publish in your name, you're taught that you really need to get credit because that's how you move up the academic ladder. And that's not how you succeed [in government], especially at the sort of junior to midlevel at these government jobs, where credit seeking undermines impact." Reuben Brigety relates that one of his greatest successes as ambassador to the African Union was galvanizing the continent's response to the 2014 outbreak of Ebola by persuading key African diplomats to do something unprecedented: "They declared a health crisis a threat to peace and security on the African continent. This gave them the legal justification to use the peace and security apparatus to help flood the [infected] zone with health care workers. . . . And we spent the next several months helping to support the African Union, and our fingerprints were gone. They got all the credit, them and USAID."

If you prefer to work on your own or in small teams, there are roles in the policy sphere for you that can mirror in many ways the academic work environment, such as private consultancies, some think tanks, and federally funded research and development centers, although many projects in the latter institutions are larger group writing projects. Some team-based work in the policy space can resemble a multiauthor study in academia; one example might be the National Intelligence Council's work to produce the wide-ranging analysis in the every-four-years *Global Trends* reports.[4] In generating such products, however, authors must subsume their own research agendas under the needs of their audience and must be wide open to edits from a host of supervisors and colleagues. Robert Kahn says he knew that he would "not enjoy the very solitary lifestyle of a researcher." He adds, "I thrived more in a communal, problem-solving team environment, and that was a judgment I made about myself."

In the largest policy organizations, like agencies of the federal government, creating change and inserting new ideas is almost never about individuals whose blinding insights override the old ways of doing things and establish new ones. Dafna Rand adds, "You really succeed again and again, if you can give your ideas to others, and if you care about impact. If you really want to change policy, the best way to do it is to work from the bottom up, give your ideas generously, sharing them with those around you, and get other people to bring up your ideas across various settings. You don't have to be in the room when people share a paradigm you have offered, . . . and sometimes it can be hard for people who have been trained to be personally connected to their ideas that the goal is instead to . . . pepper the institution with your ideas and then things will happen. It feels like a huge leap of faith for a lot of people."

If you are moved by the harmony of each part contributing to the whole, if you like combining forces with colleagues who offer different kinds of knowledge and skills to a shared project, and if you relish working with the esprit de corps generated by collective labor, then you may find happiness working within a policy office at the departments of State, Defense, or Treasury; you might enjoy a role in a mission-driven NGO engaged in policy analysis and/or advocacy; or you might be a good contributor to a team at a defense contractor like General Dynamics, working alongside scientists to develop innovative solutions to meet the needs of US military clients. For instance, after receiving his PhD in economics from MIT, Kahn declined a couple of academic offers and took a position with the Federal Reserve Board to pursue his public policy interests. During his career, he has served at the US Department of the Treasury, the International Monetary

Fund, and the World Bank; has spent time as a senior fellow at the Council on Foreign Relations; and has worked in the private sector at Citigroup, Moore Capital Management, and today at Eurasia Group, where he is director for global macroeconomics.

Am I More Motivated by Answering a Question / Solving a Puzzle or by Working to Fulfill a Vision or Mission?

By and large, the dominant orientation in the social sciences is positivism: eschewing normative commitments and making assessments and judgments based on the facts, wherever they lead. Of course, many policymakers will also insist that they're driven by facts and practical realities, not ideals—and yet scholars of foreign policy know well that normative assumptions and normative commitments are deeply enmeshed in foreign policy decisions and the policy debates that surround them. And, at a minimum, working in the government or in an organization that supports the government's work means acquiescing to and seeking to advance the government's own definition of its interests and objectives. This can be especially challenging for career executive branch officials, because each US presidential administration brings its own priorities and seeks to diffuse them across the government. Career officials must work within those parameters.

In considering a policy-focused career, you need to recognize that politics will shape the environment in which you work, at times creating personal dilemmas. Consider Erin Simpson's reflections about working with the military and the distinction she draws between the ethical responsibility she felt as an early career professional doing that work as compared with the ethical responsibility of senior Pentagon leaders:

> By the time I was at RAND, and subsequent to that, we were losing these wars [in Iraq and Afghanistan]. Americans were dying, I thought sort of unnecessarily. Iraqis were certainly dying unnecessarily. I thought it was important to try to figure out how to do this better, because I thought losing wars was bad. . . . I don't mind working with the military. I actually like working with the military in a lot of ways, but I also think it's important to help. They're going to do what they're going to do. I don't have a lot

of guilt about trying to find ways for them to do it better. Senior leadership is a different question. A lot of the work we did, I think, made these wars seem more palatable, or that they could be done in a soft sort of way or a softer way and that was less good.

Normative questions are inescapable in policy—but that doesn't mean that you must abandon your focus on objective analysis to do policy work. If you prefer to remain apart from normative questions, while recognizing and addressing the ways they manifest in the phenomena you're examining, then you're probably going to be more comfortable staying on the analytic side of the policy world. You will want to carefully consider whether the institution you go to work for is likewise committed to positivist approaches to analysis, independence of perspective, and following the facts wherever they lead.

If, by contrast, your commitment to applied work is infused with normative commitments, or if you are drawn to working toward a particular vision of the future alongside others, then you should look for work in organizations that share your values and/or vision. You might find that shared purpose in a government agency with a mission you believe in or leadership you admire; you might find it in an NGO whose policy reform agenda speaks to your values; you might even find it on a team at a private company that has a strong vision for its work, like a tech start-up or a defense corporation with an innovative idea. What you may find is that your sense of purpose is shaped by the people who surround you as much as by the organization's mission or values.

We will return to the issue of normative commitments and ethical challenges in policy work in chapter 7.

Notes

1. Paul C. Avey, Michael C. Desch, Eric Parajon, Susan Peterson, Ryan Powers, and Michael J. Tierney, "Does Social Science Inform Foreign Policy? Evidence from a Survey of US National Security, Trade, and Development Officials," *International Studies Quarterly* 66, no. 1 (2022), doi:https://academic.oup.com/isq/advance-article-abstract/doi/10.1093/isq/sqab057/6321904.

2. Susan Basalla and Maggie Debelius, *So What Are You Going to Do with That?*

Finding Careers Outside of Academia, 3rd ed. (Chicago: University of Chicago Press, 2021), 47.

3. Basalla and Debelius, chap. 2.

4. See, e.g., Office of the Director of National Intelligence, "Global Trends 2040," https://www.dni.gov/index.php/gt2040-home.

4

The Foreign Policy Ecosystem

Foreign policy in Washington does not spring fully formed, like Athena, from the seventh floor of the State Department's Harry S Truman Building; rather, it is the product of a complex set of interactions between organizations and actors, both inside and outside government. Jobs on Capitol Hill focus on legislation, whereas at the State Department, officials manage relations with other countries and international organizations on issues such as arms control or combating corruption. But policy jobs are much more expansive than the legislative and executive branches. Direct service organizations work to benefit a particular population, whereas issue advocacy organizations seek to shape the government's rules and practices on certain issues like human rights and refugees. The private sector is actively trying to understand and influence the policy environment that shapes its business environment. Washington is also host to key international organizations, such as the International Monetary Fund and the World Bank, which have their own missions and cultures.

The Washington policy world includes a range of policy-relevant functions. There are policy workers who *analyze* global events; *formulate* policy ideas; *explain, discuss, and/or debate* policy ideas with public audiences; or seek to *persuade* decision-makers. There are those who *decide* on policy choices, those who *implement* policies, and those who *assess and learn from* policy interventions that have been undertaken. There are some institutions that specialize in only one of these functions—for example, the intelligence community analyzes issues and events but never prescribes or recommends policy options. But many other institutions in the policy ecosystem, from news media to think tanks to embassies, carry out multiple functions. In more senior roles, both in and outside government, you might end up observing and analyzing events, formulating ideas, debating options, persuading key constituencies, explaining policy to the public, and implementing it through personal diplomacy—all in a single day.

In the pages that follow, we describe the major components of the Washington-based policy ecosystem, illustrating the various kinds of organizations, how they interact, and what types of work they do. In appendix B, we include a selected list of organizations illustrative of the breadth of what's available if you are looking for something research-focused: these include for-profit institutions, nonprofit think tanks, federally funded research and development centers, institutions receiving federal appropriations, and government think tanks. It's a much larger ecosystem than most people realize. The bottom line: no matter what your skill set, preferred work style, or area of substantive expertise, there is a wide range of workplaces in the policy ecosystem where you might find a fulfilling career.

There are some institutions, both in and outside government, where you can happily work for several decades, taking on different issue areas or changing job locations and gaining responsibility over time. You'll also meet many happy and successful policy practitioners who have moved among these various institutions, both in and outside government, over the course of their careers. A scholar may come into the government as a political appointee, having worked on a presidential campaign; when that administration ends, they may take their policy experience and relationships into an analytic role at a think tank, an advocacy role, or a management role at an NGO, until their political party is back in power and another political appointment becomes possible.

Obviously, the primary decision-makers in US foreign policy are in the executive branch, led by the president and the other members of the National Security Council, whose work is informed by the vast intelligence community. Congress also plays a key role in foreign policy decision-making, including appropriating foreign assistance and structuring the executive branch's conduct of policy through legislation, and members rely on their staffs as well as researchers at the Congressional Research Service. (Because the American judiciary has no foreign policy–specific infrastructure, we do not address it here, even though Supreme Court rulings can, e.g., have implications for foreign policy and national security when they touch on issues like human rights and climate change.) Related to these two decision-making branches of government are other players—both for-profit and nonprofit—that seek to inform, influence, and/or implement government policies, and actors that seek to interpret and translate policy debates and decisions for the public. These include think tank scholars, contractors, and consulting firms.

The Executive Branch

Foreign policy work within the executive branch is concentrated in several major agencies, to which PhDs often turn first when looking for policy work: the State Department, the US Agency for International Development, the Defense Department, and the intelligence community. (We discuss the intelligence community in a separate section below.)

But there are also foreign policy jobs far beyond these traditional national-security agencies. For instance, the Commerce Department has the Foreign Commercial Service which is comparable to the State Department's Foreign Service, and which deploys employees to embassies abroad as well as joining trade negotiations (which are usually led by the Office of the US Trade Representative, an arm of the White House). The Department of Labor has the Office of International Affairs, which combats child labor and human trafficking, enforces labor provisions in international trade agreements, and represents the United States to international organizations on labor issues, among other roles.

The Treasury Department includes an entire division, the Office of International Affairs, focused on international finance, markets, and development. Meanwhile, its Office of Terrorism and Financial Intelligence is responsible for researching, proposing, implementing, and enforcing sanctions against state and nonstate actors and working with international partners and the rest of the US government to reduce the financial access of terrorist groups and international criminal organizations.

The Justice Department likewise has a robust set of functions that rely on international engagement and expertise, from counterintelligence to international criminal investigations to the negotiation of mutual legal assistance treaties with other countries to make possible things like the legal extradition of suspected criminals. And, of course, the Justice Department is the US government's liaison with Interpol, the International Criminal Police Organization. Justice's International Criminal Investigative Training Assistance Program also partners closely with the US Department of State, the US Agency for International Development, and the US Department of Defense.

If you are coming out of graduate school or an academic job with specific technical skills, such as spatial science or data science skills, there are jobs across the foreign affairs agencies and intelligence community that can make use of these skills. Wesley Reisser notes, "There are what I would call technical geographers, people who work in spatial sciences and GIS [Geographic Information Systems], and they're really great practitioners with these tools. . . . There's a lot of PhD geographers working in these spaces, places like the NGA [National Geospatial-Intelligence Agency], the CIA; we have a couple within the Bureau of Intelligence and Research [at the State Department] and a whole GIS team that works here now."

Individuals working in policy offices write and coordinate documents by working with all other relevant offices. If you are an action officer at an agency like the State Department, much of your time is spent trying to coordinate among other offices with "equities." For example, let's say you are working on the Russia Desk in the European and Eurasian Affairs Bureau, and your focus is arms control. (Or it was when there were serious prospects for arms control.) You can't just push your own agenda. Other offices within State, like those overseen by the undersecretary of state for arms control and international security affairs, or perhaps the Policy Planning Staff, will have an interest in the policy options you may be working on. Then there are other agencies, like the Department of Defense and the intelligence agencies, that have their own ideas. If you need funds for arms control verification, then budgetary issues come to the fore.

This book cannot describe the full range of international affairs jobs in the executive branch, because that range is wide and also dynamic. We encourage you to explore government websites, attend in-person and virtual government job fairs, and conduct informational interviews to learn more about opportunities at specific agencies and to begin to demystify the hiring process. We encourage you to consult a companion volume to this one, also published by Georgetown University Press, *Careers in International Affairs*.[1]

Entering the Executive Branch

As you consider executive branch opportunities, it's important to understand that not all government jobs offer the same flexibility and job security that we associate with the federal Civil Service. There are several different pathways into the executive branch that are available to PhDs. Let's discuss how they differ in process, career progression, job security, and employment duration.

The process for seeking, applying for, and securing government employment is notoriously opaque, as perhaps symbolized most concretely by the byzantine website known as USAJOBS. But speaking broadly, there are several basic ways to enter government service, each with different rules, career progressions, and job security:

- the US Foreign Service (this is in the State Department; several other agencies also have their own foreign service corps),
- the Civil Service,
- various types of excepted services (notably Schedule B, experts; and Schedule C, political appointees),
- personal service contracts, and
- temporary positions, such as fellowships/internships (in some cases feeding into permanent positions), Intergovernmental Personnel Agreements, and Special Government Employees.

For more on the basic parameters of the Civil Service and excepted service categories (including Schedule B and Schedule C), see the Congressional Research Service's *Report on Categories of Federal Civil Service Employment: A Snapshot*.[2]

As a career path, the US Foreign Service is similar in certain ways to the US military: When you sign up, you commit to working within a unique community in which job assignments and career progression are highly structured according to the needs of the agency. These careers require frequent moves and years away from friends and family, and they often demand flexibility and creativity in taking on work that's outside your prior experience. Like the military, your ability to win the promotions, assignments, and professional development opportunities you seek will depend not only on your documented job performance but also on your in-service mentors and personal network as well as your "hallway reputation," meaning your demonstrated collegiality. The Foreign Service provides unique benefits: novelty, globe-spanning opportunities, the fellowship of the members of this small specialized service corps, and structured support for family members (though many officers will caution that this support can be insufficient for some families' needs). The State Department and USAID are perhaps the best-known Foreign Service employers, but depending on your interests and subject expertise, you might also consider the Commerce Department's Foreign Commercial Service or the Agriculture Department's Foreign Agricultural Service. If you're interested in joining the US Foreign Service, we encourage you to consult Harry Kopp and John Naland's *Career Diplomacy*.[3]

The US Civil Service is the largest, most flexible, and most secure form of regular employment within the US government. Once tenured into the Civil Service (a process far easier and faster than academic tenure, basically requiring three years of satisfactory service), you will have more labor protections than most private-sector employees and the ability in principle to move among the wide array of federal agencies and even to work in other parts of the country as well as abroad while retaining your rank and benefits. The highest ranks of the Civil Service are in the Senior Executive Service, whose members have demonstrated skills as leaders and managers as well as made substantive contributions to the work of their agencies.

In many federal agencies, civil servants make up the vast majority of foreign policy workers. In the State Department and USAID, many bureaus rely on civil servants not only for administrative and management roles but also for substantive expertise, especially but not exclusively in functional issue areas such as arms control, climate science, human rights, and economic affairs. The State Department offers fewer opportunities for senior civil servants than some other agencies because of its emphasis on placing Foreign Service officers in its most senior roles. That said, in recent years, Senior Executive Service members have achieved unprecedented heights in the State Department and thus have been appointed to Senate-confirmed roles as assistant secretaries for regional bureaus and as ambassadors to major US partners like Mexico and Kuwait.

Working in a Civil Service job can be both challenging and rewarding. And searching for, competing for, and acquiring a Civil Service job is itself a notoriously complex process, governed by a plethora of rules and regulations that overlay the formal system of competitive evaluation. All Civil Service jobs, whether they are open to applicants from outside the government or not, are posted on USAJOBS, the federal government's central portal for employment. Generally speaking, you must submit your application for a Civil Service role through USAJOBS, and applications are screened by human resources professionals and/or an automated process before any are reviewed by the office that is actually hiring.

You may have heard advice like, "If you're not a veteran, don't bother applying" or "If you want your application to get through the USAJOBS screening, you have to hire a consultant to rewrite your résumé." There may be grains of truth in such advice, but the reality is far less categorical. There are many free resources available to help potential applicants navigate the USAJOBS application system; we recommend starting with the Partnership for Public Service's comprehensive Go Government website.[4] In addition, there are pathways into the Civil Service that are designed specifically for those with graduate degrees, such as the Presidential Management Fellowship (PMF).

We know many, many individuals in Washington with graduate degrees who have gone into government agencies on their two-year PMF fellowship and stayed on in public service. Fellows, who receive salary and benefits through the program, have opportunities to do two or three rotations in different offices and potentially even in more than one federal agency, thereby giving the fellow exposure to a range of opportunities. The annual application process runs through USAJOBS and is highly competitive. Since a master's degree from an accredited institution is a sufficient prerequisite, students who are in a PhD program might become eligible as soon as they get a master's along the way, as is the case in many programs. Applicants can apply if they have received their advanced degree within the past two years or if they will receive the degree by August 31 of the year after they begin the application process, and individuals can apply to the program more than once as long as they remain eligible. Veterans who are unable to apply within two years of receiving their degree because of military service obligations have up to six years to apply to a separate program, known as the Recent Graduates Program.[5]

A more focused opportunity is the John S. McCain Strategic Defense Fellows Program, which requires a master's degree or above to work in the Office of the Secretary of Defense or an office of the secretary of a military department for one year. The purpose is, through mentorship from senior leaders, to "gain [Department of Defense] experience and leadership capabilities through challenging opportunities to flourish into problem solvers, strategic thinkers and future leaders."[6]

Federal agencies can also make use of "excepted service" hiring authorities to fill out their staff with needed expertise (Schedule B) and to bring in senior advisers identified by the White House to help advance the president's policy agenda (Schedule C). In both cases, these jobs are not generally publicly posted or have an open application, but require you to have some direct engagement with the hiring authorities (the White House's Presidential Personnel Office in the case of Schedule C, and the specific office or agency doing the hiring for Schedule B). These roles do not offer the same job security as either Civil Service or Foreign Service roles. Schedule B employees can serve for up to two years, renewable once (up to four years total); Schedule C employees serve "at the pleasure of the president," meaning that they can be fired at any time, and they are expected to submit their resignations when a new president takes office. Schedule B and Schedule C employees are given a rank and salary based on the Civil Service scales. In practice, many administrations use Schedule B as well as Schedule C to bring policy experts affiliated with their political and policy preferences into government.

There are also opportunities for established scholars seeking to do a temporary stint in public service. The Council on Foreign Relations and the American Association for the Advancement of Science offer one-year fellowships that give scholars an opportunity to engage in practice to enhance research and teaching by improving their understanding of the policy process. But there are other pathways into government, such as working on a presidential campaign and then being hired as Schedule B or Schedule C appointees to provide expertise to agencies like the National Security Council and the State Department. In some cases, scholars can go into the government through the Intergovernmental Personnel Act program, under which their university agrees to pay the faculty member while they are working in government; this gives government additional expertise and allows universities to enable their faculty members to perform public service.

Contractors

Many private companies provide staffing and services to federal agencies under contract. Service contractors work across the federal government, although many of the companies that provide these staff members specialize in certain issue areas, skill sets, or federal agencies. Some service contractors provide training or support to federal offices in information technology, administration, custodial services, security, and other areas; others provide highly skilled workers to undertake tasks such as data analysis, research, and program management. If you offer specialized skills, such as foreign language research capabilities or program evaluation, you can also find longer-term work for a government service contractor that markets you for short-term projects across agencies and offices.

Personal Service Contractors (PSCs) are people who work in the federal government and are directly supervised by US government personnel but are not themselves civil servants. These contractors allow agencies to add to their workforces in a more flexible manner when needed. If you are a PSC employee working at a place like the State Department or USAID, your day-to-day work experience, and even your job duties, might be identical to those of a Civil Service colleague sitting at the desk next door. But your employment terms are not the same and your salary and benefits may not match those of your government-employee colleagues. And if the project you're working on ends, if funding is cut, or if needs change, you might find yourself unemployed or shifted by your employer to another worksite.

It is possible to start work in a federal agency as a PSC, build your skills and your networks, and then transition into an "adjacent" Civil Service position by demonstrating the knowledge and competencies to compete successfully through USAJOBS. And, if nothing else, time as a PSC can offer you direct insight into what a given federal workplace is like and help you build your network, advancing your thinking about your preferences for federal employment.

The Intelligence Community

Working for a US intelligence agency, or in an intelligence role inside a federal agency, is a specialized subset of executive branch foreign policy work. Intelligence work is focused on giving policymakers and policy implementers the information and analysis they need to do their jobs well. If you work in intelligence, you design your work product around the needs of your "customer," whether that is a military combatant commander or the president of the United States. But while the intelligence community offers analysis and prediction, it specifically abjures making policy recommendations. Thus, for example, the National Security Council has cabinet officers, the president, and the vice president as members, but the director of national intelligence and the chairman of the Joint Chiefs of Staff are not members but "statutory advisers."[7]

The intelligence community has a unique culture of policy analysis, given its access to classified information and its role in the policy process. Most analytic products go through a rigorous review, including peer feedback and solicitation and incorporation of views from teams with different perspectives and areas of expertise than the authors. Some analytic products are deliberately "red-teamed"— challenged by competing analysis to reveal relative weaknesses in the foundational evidence or reasoning and to highlight key areas of debate. Other analytic products, like national intelligence estimates, are designed to communicate a consensus across the intelligence community, but they also include clearly indicated points of dispute among different intelligence agencies. This rigor and transparency is designed to maximize the client's confidence in the analysis presented, while making clear what is not known.

Zoe Danon, who has spent a dozen years in the intelligence community, says that the work took her research skills from graduate school to a new level: "I learned to do research as a PhD student, and to really look at things, to do a deep dive into a topic and stick with it, to have a lot of revisions and a lot of people weighing in on what I was doing." In the intelligence community, she relates, she learned "clear thinking. Figuring out: what is the key question? What do I need to answer it? What does my audience need—they don't need everything that I have learned in this process. What do they need to know, and how do I best lay it out for them?" Intelligence analysts are also trained in swift, clear, and concise writing—a skill that many find valuable in careers when they leave the intelligence community.

Most agencies within the intelligence community typically post their vacancies for specific jobs on USAJOBS (and make sure to look at https://www.intelligencecareers.gov/) as well as on their organization's websites (such as https://www.cia.gov/careers/jobs/); there are pockets of the intelligence community where jobs are posted only on the organization's website. In some cases, there are virtual career fairs for which applicants go through USAJOBS, and then, if deemed of interest, they get invited to the career fair that is outside the USAJOBS process. There are also agencies recruiting through sites like Handshake, and, as in other cases, once the application is processed through the site, the remainder of the process takes place via emails and phone calls.

The Legislative Branch

Although the president is seen as the preeminent actor in the US government on foreign policy, Congress also plays an important role in appropriations, advice and consent, and much more. Members of Congress rely on foreign policy advisers in their own congressional offices as well as those who staff congressional committees covering intelligence, armed services, foreign affairs, and "Foreign Operations" (the appropriations subcommittee responsible for overseeing funding for foreign affairs programs).

Foreign policy advisers to individual members of Congress some-times have doctoral degrees, and many have master's degrees. But typically, their skill set is as much in politics and the legislative process as it is in foreign affairs. For example, Paul Bonicelli is the national security adviser to Senator Rick Scott (R) of Florida. Bonicelli is a political scientist and served in the US Agency for International Development, but he built his congressional connections by working on political campaigns in the years after college. In graduate school, he says, "I didn't do any politics, but I stayed in touch with these people, my friends. I would come up and visit and we would write or talk on the phone. . . . And they were continuing in their careers, progressing, getting married, having kids, and continuing in that path on the Hill. Some worked for Reagan, of course, some worked for George H. W. [Bush]." His first congressional role, after writing a dissertation on democracy in Mexico, was on the House Foreign Affairs Committee's Subcommittee on Western Hemisphere Affairs. He notes that his "committee dealt with development, democracy, and drugs. We did a lot with Colombia and Central America." Bonicelli's experience highlights a key element of working on foreign policy on Capitol Hill: the sheer breadth of issues one is expected to cover.

The key congressional foreign policy committees have separate Republican and Democratic professional staffs, with up to a dozen advisers who divide up the committee's subject matter responsibility along regional, functional, or other lines. These staff members carry out the core of congressional oversight for their respective federal agencies, reviewing congressional notifications, taking executive briefings, and traveling to observe US government operations abroad. These staff members also support their members of Congress in organizing hearings, drafting bills and managing them through the legislative process, and vetting presidential nominees for senior executive roles to prepare for the Senate's exercise of its advice-and-consent role. Committee staff members also occasionally undertake major research to produce reports on topics of special interest to their committee's leadership. Recent examples include Senate Select Committee on Intelligence's reports on CIA torture in the "war on terrorism" and on Russian interference in the 2016 presidential election.

The Congressional Research Service (CRS) is probably the largest congressional employer of experts in international affairs. CRS, part of the Library of Congress, is a rigorously nonpartisan source of research and analysis for congressional offices. Any congressional office can make a confidential query to CRS, which will assign relevant staff members to answer it in confidence. In addition, CRS prepares reports, briefings, and seminars on a wide array of policy topics for congressional staff members to use in their work. CRS prides itself on work that is confidential, authoritative, objective, and nonpartisan.[8] Like the executive branch's intelligence community, CRS analysts never provide policy recommendations—instead, they offer congressional offices information and analysis, context such as history and trends in a policy area, and the questions that are before Congress on the issue. Zoe Danon, now research coordinator for the foreign affairs and defense team at CRS, notes that "we try to really, without our own bias, lay out and give a good rendering of the debates that are going on. And then, to the extent that there are proposals under debate, we try to give a sense of the possible outcomes to consider including both the goals of a policy, but also maybe some unintended consequences that could come up." CRS researchers also produce public reports on important current topics.[9]

There are fellowships designed to bring PhDs into the legislative branch for brief stints, such as the American Political Science Association's Congressional Fellowship. (Some recipients of the Council on Foreign Relations' International Affairs Fellowship have also taken their yearlong opportunity up on Capitol Hill.) These placements can be on committee staffs as well as in members' personal offices.

Nonprofit Organizations: Direct-Service and Issue Advocacy

The nonprofit sector includes a wide range of organizations (e.g., most think tanks are also nonprofits). But there are two types of organizations that most PhDs don't immediately think of when they consider foreign policy workplaces: direct service NGOs and issue-advocacy NGOs.

Direct service NGOs use voluntary contributions and government grants to provide services to people and organizations abroad. Examples include humanitarian relief groups like Mercy Corps, wide-ranging education and development organizations like IREX, and smaller, specialized groups like the International Center for Not-for-Profit Law. These organizations rely on experts to design projects, to implement them, and to evaluate them for best practices and lessons learned that can be applied to future work. In addition, many of these organizations have staff members in Washington who work directly on government policy related to their area of work. Mercy Corps, for example, has an analysis team in its Washington policy office to develop policy recommendations based on its own experience and then to advocate for policy changes that it believes will help the whole humanitarian services sector.

Issue advocacy NGOs do just what this name describes: they engage policymakers, opinion shapers like the media, and the public to push policy outcomes in the direction they wish to see. They may be built around communities of interest in a particular region or concern (e.g., the Washington Office on Latin America), or a coalition of like-minded organizations (e.g., the US Chamber of Commerce), or they may be an organization with a nationwide, grassroots membership (e.g., the Armenian Assembly of America). In order to advocate effectively for their issues and policy preferences, it's essential for these organizations to have a sophisticated understanding of the policies they care about, how those policies are developed and carried out within legal and government institutions, and how those policies affect the countries, individuals, and communities of concern to them. Advocacy organizations can range from small groups with very few permanent staff members—for example, the Project on Middle East Democracy—to large, wealthy organizations that undertake in-house research to advance their arguments for policy change, like AARP. Many core American civil society organizations, such as unions and churches, have Washington policy offices that do at least some foreign policy advocacy work of importance to their memberships. The policy office staff may be small in number, but they are backed by large grassroots memberships whose advocacy can reach hundreds of members of Congress.

Many organizations undertake both direct service work and advocacy in their issue area and view both activities as central components of advancing their mission or supporting their core constituency.

Think Tanks

Think tanks play a number of roles in the policy ecosystem. They translate insights from academia into policy-relevant ideas for government.[10] They offer a platform for both public and private dialogue between policymakers and other interested parties, including advocates, media, and foreign actors (through so-called track two dialogues). They offer independent expert analysis and advice to Congress, the executive branch, the intelligence community, and the wider public. And because they focus on both the substance and the process of policymaking, think tanks can derive generalizable knowledge about policy questions in a way that is more relevant to and operationalizable for policy actors than can most academics. And because their scholars gain a public profile and operate daily alongside or even in collaboration with political candidates, parties, and campaigns in close-knit Washington, they are also a primary source of political appointees for presidential administrations.

Most think tanks are nonprofit institutions, where fundraising from foundation, corporate, and individual donors is a key skill alongside research and communication. Some think tanks are declaratively nonpartisan, while others have affiliations with a political party, movement, or ideological tendency. Think tanks also differ in who they see as their primary audience and the range of written products they value. The Brookings Institution's senior fellow, Tanvi Madan, notes "how much diversity there is across various organizations, even within think tanks. At a place like Brookings, you're not going to get to be a senior fellow until you have a book. Many think tanks wouldn't care about that; they might care more about things like op-eds."

Like most academic institutions, some think tanks invest in the notion that the depth of knowledge and credibility that derives from peer-reviewed, book-length research is an unparalleled asset in policy debates. Writing books also requires that the time horizon for your work's impact is longer—and your project must be designed for longer-term relevance, tackling perennial issues or major trends in foreign policy. But think tanks can also have impact by helping audiences that must cover a wide range of issues, like news media and congressional staff, understand swiftly moving events in a given area. Thus, op-eds, briefing papers of one to two thousand words, podcasts, and other short-form products can also be valued products to provide context for and interpret events in the headlines.

Included within the universe of think tanks are a subset of federally funded research and development centers (FFRDCs), which also include national laboratories like Los Alamos and Lawrence Livermore, which offer postdoctoral fellowships, and MITRE, which is a systems engineering FFRDC. The FFRDCs that function more or less as think tanks are the RAND Corporation, the Center for Naval Analyses (CNA), and the Institute for Defense Analyses (IDA). Of these, RAND undertakes privately funded research in addition to government-funded projects, while IDA and CNA largely rely on the government's project funding. These institutions mostly undertake research geared to answer questions for a specific client, and their research products may or may not be publicly released. Unlike a consulting firm such as McKinsey or Booz Allen, however, FFRDCs pride themselves on undertaking their research with independence and reporting their findings without fear or favor. Unlike at some think tanks, where scholars are often (but not always) working on sole-authored projects, FFRDCs typically have team-based reports with multiple authors; so once again, it's important to understand how you like to work as you think about what types of opportunities to pursue. An advantage of working at an FFRDC is that because their reports are commissioned, they will be produced for, and consumed by, the client. (If it is a classified report, sometimes an unclassified version will be published.) In academia, not all work submitted for publication gets past the review process.

The Private Sector

The corporate world includes many organizations with international activities and business stakes in international politics. ExxonMobil, Facebook, and General Dynamics are all examples of private-sector actors with global interests that engage regularly in foreign policy debates in Washington as well as in their own interactions with foreign governments and other international interlocutors. For all these reasons, they seek out and employ experts in international affairs. An increasing number of PhDs with training in statistical methods, for-mal modeling, and other data science skills are finding employment in the private sector. Among those we spoke with, Robert Kahn, Jennifer McArdle, Morgan Kaplan, Erin Simpson, and Paul McLachlan have all put their skills to work in the private sector across a range of insti-tutions, including, in the case of McLachlan, outside the foreign pol-icy world in Silicon Valley. In chapter 6, we profile Simpson, who in addition to her government work helped build a start-up and became director of strategy development and deployment, space systems, at Northrop Grumman.

To make his transition to the private sector, Morgan Kaplan says, "The first step [was] literally just to know what's out there." Friends in academia who made the transition ahead of him helped, such as a graduate school colleague who introduced him to consulting. Kaplan went to a recruiting event, and "they kept talking about using hypoth-eses, and how they use data to answer hypotheses." He realized he could do this type of work because he was, in fact, "trained to answer questions." We've discussed the importance of networks in this book; Kaplan says that to understand the private sector, he reached back to friends from childhood to help him navigate a landscape he did not know before he started.

A major challenge, Kaplan says, is translating how the skill set you developed in academia is directly applicable to nonacademic jobs. Talking about your PhD as five years of work experience leading to what the position entails is important. Some companies understand this, but others do not. Kaplan got hired into his current job in the technology sector to "work with the experts at my company on thought leadership." Similar to his previous work as a journal editor, his job in part is to help "curate ideas to help make them stronger, and, most importantly, help communicate them to a wider public."

Eurasia Group, where Robert Kahn works, engages in political risk analysis and consulting for major corporations and financial institu-tions, and includes a number of PhDs, particularly in political sci-ence.[11] Kahn says that at his firm, there is a "stature that comes from knowing the language of thought leadership. So to be a PhD, to be able to talk big ideas and frame the debates and contribute to them at that level, is something that is highly valued." He adds that in addition to analytical and writing abilities, which are critical skills in so many workplaces, at Eurasia Group, so is "the ability to construct thoughtful narratives around public policy debates." The political scientists at the firm can tell a story about political trends, and the economists can tell the story of the impact on markets and particularly economic sectors. They aren't just producing reports for any interested client to read; they are coming up with tailored advice for clients looking to understand the effects of policies for their investment decisions.

It's not just the work that Kahn finds interesting; it's also the environment: "Let's say you are a PhD in political science, and you have the opportunity to come to Eurasia Group, you're going to be in an environment with a critical mass of other advanced political science thinkers, which allows for both a stimulating environment that would be different than if you were the only political scientist at a consulting company doing X. Every day, you would come to a morning meeting and you'd get in arguments with your colleagues, and that would be stimulating."

One of the features about the private-sector jobs he has held that Kahn has enjoyed is the diversity of expertise around him, something that McArdle and McLachlan mentioned to us as well. "If you come to a place like Citigroup, which was my first private sector job," Kahn reflects, "you might be a researcher, but you're sitting at a desk next to a physicist, and a trader, and an MBA, and that diversity of skill set is, at a well-managed private institution, a positive. It creates an innovative laboratory that is quite interesting to someone like me."

Other Career Options in the Ecosystem

There are other career options that support work in the policy realm. Private foundations, for example, which can shape academic fields, are also major funders of foreign policy work both in Washington and in the field. There are legacy foundations like the Carnegie Corporation of New York and the Ford Foundation with billions of dollars in assets and a vast array of both analytic and programmatic projects. There are also new, but massive, foundations with a keen interest in international work, like the Bill & Melinda Gates Foundation. The funds that the Gates Foundation puts into global public health and gender equality, for example, probably rival those of many governments. A new generation of wealthy individuals, primarily but not exclusively located in Silicon Valley, are drawing on their significant resources to support causes they care about, like the Chan-Zuckerberg Initiative and the Schmidt Family Foundation. Some foundations are exclusively funders; some are both grantmaking and "operating" foundations—meaning that they carry out their own self-funded projects in areas from nuclear security to human development. Still others are dedicated operating foundations that may fund other organizations to partner with them but do not work primarily through grantmaking.

PhDs working at foundations can have a tremendous impact on academia and on policy. We spoke with two such individuals, Stephen Del Rosso at the Carnegie Corporation of New York and William Ruger, who worked previously at the Charles Koch Institute (CKI) and Charles Koch Foundation (CKF). Del Rosso wanted to build better connections between academia and policy, and with the support of longtime Carnegie Corporation president Vartan Gregorian, he helped generate a host of university-based programs designed to "bridge the gap" between these worlds; Carnegie has also supported a range of other efforts, including media platforms like *The Conversation* and *The Monkey Cage* that publish the work of scholars seeking to connect with the policy world. Ruger used his perch at CKI and CKF to build up the voices of those calling for a more "restrained" US foreign policy by supporting the creation of centers and faculty/scholar positions at a number of universities and think tanks designed to develop more research and writing in this area. There are other PhDs who have built major programs at philanthropic organizations. Emma Belcher, currently the president of the Ploughshares Fund, worked for nearly a decade at the John D. and Catherine T. MacArthur Foundation, where she built that organization's Nuclear Challenge Big Bet team, which at that time operated with a $20 million budget.[12] Given the trends toward specialization in many fields, Del Rosso told us that there are an increasing number of employers in the philanthropic world with a preference for PhDs that could provide some rewarding opportunities to shape both research and practice on issues you care about.

Outside of foundations, there are also editor positions at journals like *International Security* or *The Washington Quarterly* or at university presses that can keep you connected to scholarship in a very direct way, helping to shape what gets published in your field. While these are not faculty positions, like work at foundations, they provide individuals with opportunities to shape academic fields as well as to contribute to the policy discourse. These positions can also be important vehicles for increasing diversity, equity, and inclusion in both spheres by bringing a range of new voices into the debates. As the executive editor of *International Security* from 2019 to 2021, Morgan Kaplan made a conscious effort to encourage early career scholars who might not have thought their work was relevant to the journal to discuss their articles with him for possible submission. He also created a podcast—*IS: Off the Page*—that enabled scholars to discuss their work directly with practitioners and hopefully to then have a direct impact with their findings.

While this book focuses primarily on the foreign policy ecosystem in Washington, as we have just seen, there are also opportunities in other parts of the United States. These include the work at foundations, journals, and university presses that we have just discussed as well as places like the national laboratories in New Mexico and California or non-DC-based think tanks around the world. There are positions in international organizations in cities like New York, Geneva, Vienna, and Brussels. There are many non-foreign-policy job options for social science PhDs in Silicon Valley. And there are careers in the uniformed military and careers in state and local governments (which are increasingly engaged in international relations of their own). For more information on the various types of organizations that work in international affairs, we encourage you to consult *Careers in International Affairs*, now in its ninth edition.[13]

Notes

1. Laura E. Cressey, Barrett J. Helmer, and Jennifer E. Steffensen, eds., *Careers in International Affairs*, 9th ed. (Washington, DC: Georgetown University Press, 2014).

2. Congressional Research Service, *Categories of Federal Civil Service Employment: A Snapshot*, Report R45635, https://crsreports.congress.gov/product/pdf/R/R45635/3.

3. Harry W. Kopp and John K. Naland, *Career Diplomacy: Life and Work in*

the US Foreign Service, 4th ed. (Washington, DC: Georgetown University Press, 2021).

4. Go Government, "There's a Government Career for Everyone," no date, https://gogovernment.org/.

5. US Office of Personnel Management, "Become a Presidential Management Fellow," October 7, 2022, https://www.pmf.gov/become-a-pmf/eligibility/.

6. Washington Headquarters Services, "John S. McCain Strategic Defense Fellows Program," no date, https://www.whs.mil/mccain-fellows-program/.

7. See White House, "National Security Council," no date, https://www.whitehouse.gov/nsc/.

8. Library of Congress, "Values," November 15, 2022, https://www.loc.gov/crsinfo/about/values.html.

9. You can search for examples of CRS reports here: https://crsreports.congress.gov/.

10. For more on think tanks, see Andrew Selee, *What Should Think Tanks Do? A Strategic Guide to Policy Impact* (Stanford, CA: Stanford University Press, 2013).

11. See Eurasia Group, "Our Story," no date, https://www.eurasiagroup.net/our-story.

12. See Belcher's Ploughshares Fund biography page, https://ploughshares.org/about-us/staff-board/dr-emma-belcher.

13. Cressey, Helmer, and Steffensen, *Careers in International Affairs*.

5

Looking for a Job in Foreign Policy

As we have seen, when you are in a PhD program, there are a variety of workshops, programs, and internships that can set you up for a future policy or private-sector career. But there's a problem: Your dissertation advisers may view some of these activities as a diversion from what they think you should be doing in an academically oriented program. Most academic faculty are going to encourage you to use your summers before advancing to candidacy (i.e., finishing your coursework, exams, and prospectus defense and moving on to writing the dissertation) to work as a research assistant or to attend methods workshops, of which there are a number designed to help increase your qualitative and/or quantitative skills. And once you have advanced to candidacy, advisers will want you to focus on your research and writing. If you have field research to do, they'll want you to concentrate on the research needed for your dissertation, not work as a consultant for an outside entity that might take you away from your own project. If you are thinking about a career outside academia, however, you may have other considerations. Tanvi Madan left DC to go to graduate school and get to know a perspective from another part of the country, but she wanted to stay involved in the world she left behind. "I was still getting invited to do policy-related stuff in DC," she recalls, "and occasionally somebody at the university would say, 'You know, you're wasting time. You should be focused on your dissertation.' And to me, it wasn't [wasting time]. I did want to stay involved."

As you embark on a search for a job in foreign policy, you'll face basic questions about making the transition from academia. For example, Alexandra Evans points out that when finishing up your graduate work and looking for a job, there can be a great deal of uncertainty about financial planning. What if you finish and you don't have a job lined up? The nonacademic job market doesn't necessarily follow the academic calendar (although we saw how in economics, the job market interviews take place at the same time). And what do you do if you are applying to jobs where you will have to wait for a security clearance? Federal internships and summer programs can be good ways to initiate a clearance process or to maintain a clearance while in graduate school.

If you receive a "conditional acceptance" to a job that requires a security clearance, you may have to wait months before you can begin your employment. So you'll need to build that into your planning. You may want to look for a postdoctoral fellowship or a short-term consultancy, or perhaps your home institution can provide some kind of bridge through research or adjunct teaching to get you through that uncertain period. Matthew Jacobs had a conditional acceptance to join the intelligence community when he was offered a job at Anderson University in South Carolina, about a twenty-five-minute drive from his parents' home. His teaching load was four courses per semester. He started teaching in August 2016, and then in November he got word that his security clearance had come through. The government wanted him to start two weeks later. Jacobs told them his teaching contract went until May, and they agreed to let him start when the school year was over.

When Reuben Brigety was discharged from the Navy and finished his PhD, he had no experience with the policy job market: "I just sent out fifty letters to different organizations, saying, 'Look, I'm a great guy and you ought to hire me, and here's why.'" He ended up with two offers: one to help run a refugee camp on the Afghanistan-Pakistan border and one as an analyst in the arms division of Human Rights Watch in Washington.

Presenting Your Skill Set

As you've read in earlier chapters, the policy job market is looking for people like you—but to demonstrate your value, you need to present yourself differently than you would for an academic job. Having taken coursework, maybe done some fieldwork, and utilized the methods you were trained in to produce a dissertation, either in the form of a book-length manuscript or a set of papers, how can you best present yourself? What skills and background do you have that would appeal to an employer outside academia? Presenting yourself well for a policy role means that you must think like a policy worker: focus on your audience and what they need to fulfill their mission. Mara Revkin cautions you to keep it simple when you put together your résumé, or CV, for a policy job: "I basically have a policy version of my CV that eliminates entire sections from the academic CV. There are sections, like peer reviewer service and conference participations that are just not relevant outside academia. The CV should be really short and only include the things that would matter to them."

In fact, your graduate experience has given you many policy-relevant skills. It's not just that you have an ability to analyze large amounts of data. Teaching experience means you know how to break down complex facts and ideas and communicate them—and that means you have briefing experience. Jennifer McArdle found in the start-up world that teaching experience "gives you immediate credibility." Winning a grant, or working on a grant-funded project, or helping to put together a workshop or speaker series all show that you have project management skills. And think about your committee; was it difficult keeping those three or more academics on board with your project? Well, then, you have diplomatic skills, don't you? "One of the things that I try to emphasize," Sara Plana says, "is that I was a 'student,' but for about four of those six years I was an independent researcher. I was not in coursework. I was creating, managing, and implementing my own projects, and I think that is a skill set that people don't understand. . . . They just see that you've been in school for six years. . . . I don't think they realize that you are your own boss and you manage projects, and you often manage people in those projects; . . . as much as you can convey your practical skills for a particular job, I think that's key." And don't forget how good you are at taking notes, which can be very important for ensuring a proper record of government meetings.[1]

Your specific research skills may translate into a policy job in unexpected ways. For example, maybe you've done survey research. This is valuable for development organizations and agencies, as Mara Revkin describes: "Almost all humanitarian and development organizations do surveys of their beneficiaries or communities for needs assessments or impact evaluation, so that is a good skill to develop." Matthew Jacobs says that when he was applying to jobs in the intelligence community, he got a lot of advice about how to extract job-relevant skills from his graduate school experience: "You wrote a dissertation," they said, "so think about that as a big project you were in charge of. Did you get any research money? Well, then you managed a budget for that. Did you do international travel? Then you managed that money for international travel. With your teaching, you managed a classroom of more than one hundred students." He also learned from others what not to include. "The fact that you presented at a conference four or five years ago," he heard, "nobody cares." He mentioned he had done research in Cuba and had gone through bureaucratic processes to do research at the Cuban Foreign Ministry. His advisers told him to highlight that since other applicants wouldn't have that on their résumé.

While doing her PhD, Plana and a graduate school colleague, Rachel Tecott, worked with Kathleen Hicks at the Center for Strategic and International Studies to found the Future Strategy Forum, an annual, all-day conference that features women national security policymakers and scholars. "I've gained so much from that initiative very serendipitously, and I've learned a ton about management and a ton about event planning and sponsorship and fundraising," says Plana. But even if you don't launch a major project like that in graduate school, don't forget, she continues, that "PhDs are problem-solvers." Maybe you couldn't do the fieldwork you wanted to conduct because of COVID-19, or you had to overcome, as she puts it, "the data problems that come with most dissertations." Be prepared to describe to interviewers how you identified and overcame challenges in the process of earning your degree. In addition to letting you highlight specific skills you acquired, these anecdotes also demonstrate your creativity and persistence.

One of the ways you can learn better how to translate your skills and knowledge for nonacademic employers is to take as many interviews as you can. Morgan Kaplan notes, "Every interview, whether it's successful or not, is a learning experience on how to talk about yourself. It took many, many interviews before I learned how to speak about my experience in a way that mattered to people in the private sector."

Whatever discipline you come from, you will have been trained in certain quantitative and/or qualitative methods. But you need to learn how to talk about these skills. Alice Hunt Friend argues, "You can really parlay actual methodological training into a real asset, and so, I think the trick there is just to learn the ways that policy folks talk about training because the jargon that we use in academia does not translate, and vice versa. And so, you just have to learn the jargon on policy, which is totally learnable. I mean, go to wherever the trade press is, for whatever part of the government that you're applying to, and read enough of it to start to pick up the kinds of words and terminology that they use." Tanvi Madan notes a common mistake: "You'll see people explaining their dissertations or what they do and they will pitch it in the same way they would pitch it to a faculty recruitment committee." This is different. While you can often answer the "so what" question in academia by referring to theory and method, in the policy world, you need to demonstrate that your knowledge and skills can help solve policy problems.

One way the academic and policy worlds differ is that employers in the policy world may privilege substantive knowledge over methodological training, unlike in many academic jobs. Alice Hunt Friend remarks, "If you say, 'I lived in Kenya, and I speak a couple of Kenyan languages,' and you're applying to the Africa Bureau at State, that's really exciting. So, I think I would sort of look at what the job is, figure out what the substantive expertise is, and then really emphasize that because I will say, having been on the regional side and what we call functional side at [Defense], we were constantly looking for people who actually knew stuff about what we were studying. So, if you're a functionalist, and we were in the nuclear office, we were looking for nuclear experts out in academia, and so we don't want to know why you know these things like the whole front part of your journal article. Don't tell me about that, tell me about what the conclusion says. I will believe you if you have 'Dr.' in front of your name, I'm going to believe that your knowledge is valid. Just tell me your knowledge. I think that's probably the top thing because what 'Dr.' means to folks in policy is 'knows all the things,' not *how* they know all the things."

Wesley Reisser adds that undertaking field research also gives "a lot of cultural sensitivity, where you can go out into other parts of the world . . . with a level of cultural competence that others won't bring to the table. . . . I know a little bit about everywhere, so I always can find something to talk to a foreign interlocutor about that isn't just the business in the [briefing] paper, and they appreciate that, and they don't get that from very many American diplomats. As a geographer, I think you kind of have a little bit of a magic tool set there that you can bring in that can help just crack the door open in conversations that are hard, which is a big part of being a diplomat."

Silicon Valley—a place that hires a lot of computer programmers, engineers, and data scientists—also values project management skills if you are looking beyond the international affairs field (although many firms do have a major international presence). Paul McLachlan says that there are options in Silicon Valley, even if you "are not the best at coding in Python. That is an inaccurate perception of what the labor market is looking for. Most teams are divided into kinds of engineering, which is tech, traditionally coding work, and product management and development, which is trying to understand what stakeholders' needs are and how do you manage particular features or products." In other words, as in government, tech firms need workers who are good at problem-solving for real people in the social world.

Whatever type of job you are applying for, keep in mind, as Tanvi Madan says, a core skill is "adapting your pitch to an audience, and that means learning to understand who that audience is, and what it is that you are pitching for."

Mind-Set

In addition to framing your skill set, you also need to convince employers that you can be a team player, that you can work on projects that other people initiate, and that you are there to carry things out. It is impressive that you have been your own boss to produce a major research project, but you will likely be hired to be part of a team. Employers want to know if you can play well with others. As Mary Barton notes, "There's the stereotype that I often heard during information interviews—PhDs are hard to work with, they want their name on all the reports and papers, versus putting the mission of the office first, and a willingness to not always be acknowledged for your role. Sometimes, it's important to play against type." Similarly, Morgan Kaplan warns that many employers are wary of PhDs because they fear they will miss the autonomy of the academy and will be frustrated working on less intellectual projects. But if you are in an interview, and the person you are speaking with is speaking negatively about academics, don't take it personally: "It's not about you, but it is on you to let them know why you're interested in a nonacademic job."

A broader perspective is one of the things Dafna Rand looks for when she hires; if she's hiring people coming from academia, she wants to know, "Do they have the right temperament? Are you able to check personal ambitions and make sure that the mission and sense of substantive contribution drives every decision?" When she is hiring, she also asks, "How willing are folks who are academics to level up their findings to a broader level of analysis and generalization? Depending on people's experiences, expertise, and various life experiences, they range in how they present the findings of their research. Some academics are very good at quickly conveying the 'so what?' elements of a problem or project."

Keep in mind that while you are presenting the skills you've developed through your PhD program, you aren't necessarily getting a job based on the dissertation itself. Alexandra Evans points out, "There's an incredible amount of competition for these jobs from PhDs and non-PhDs. And your dissertation is usually not going to impress anybody. So, the thing you have worked the hardest on for years is actually the thing that you kind of need to deprioritize. And that's very difficult when you've spent years working on something you really care about and refining your one-minute, ten-minute, twenty-minute pitches about that thing. And then nobody wants to hear more than a sentence. So that's very hard."

That said, the simple act of finishing a dissertation shows, among other things, your initiative, motivation, and organization. As Steve Galpern notes, "To actually complete your PhD, I've said this to people, you don't have to be the smartest person but you do have to have a certain amount of discipline to get that done. And I think that's an enormously helpful quality in terms of being a self-starter, somebody who's self-motivated."

Think about the ways your academic discipline has taught you how to approach problems. The geographer Wesley Reisser says, "Political scientists and economists take a theoretical construct and build out from that. . . . Historians think about things through the nexus of time, and that's their approach to studying issues and exploring issues. Geographers start instead from time through the concept of space, so we ask 'Where?' first. . . . I've always urged geographers who want to come in my direction and this kind of work that your selling point is that you work on the exact same set of issues as a political scientist or an economist or a historian that also might be competing for these same jobs. The difference is that you think about things in a different way."

Meanwhile, Mary Barton, who is in an analyst position, puts her training as a historian to good use: using research and documents to tell a story. "You define the patterns in the documents," as she puts it, "and then bring those forward to tell the story, and your research has real-world implications. A lot of the skills that we're trained to do—archival research, intensive, open-source research, secondary source research, and then marshaling that all together in a compelling narrative—that's what my job is."

Writing and Communicating

There's communicating the skills you have, and then there's the communication skill itself. Can you write well? Can you give a good presentation or a crisp brief? Kori Schake says, "The two most important skills, I think, are to write pungently and succinctly; and to be able to explain in ninety seconds what's important about this problem and what do I think you should do; . . . policy people are really busy people, and most of them are really smart, good problem solvers. And so the ability to say, 'Here's what's important, and here's what I think you should do,' and let them ask you why. But mostly, if you can say, 'Here's the question, here are the three things important to answer the question, and here's what I think the answer is,' walking down a hallway in ninety seconds, that's how I made myself good at policy jobs." Mara Revkin reminds us that there's a difference between a PowerPoint for an audience of practitioners or policymakers and a PowerPoint for a political science job talk: "Just being able to communicate key findings in simple terms is really important."

If you have expertise, and you've presented your work to people both inside and outside academia at any level, then flaunt it. The historian James Graham Wilson says that when applying on the USAJOBS website, you will need to answer questions about whether you've done briefings before. You have. Maybe you've lectured and have presented your research at conferences with the world's experts on your topic sitting in the room. Maybe you've TAd for big names in your field. You've taught students. You've mentored junior TAs. As he puts it, "Yes, I am an expert recognized by other experts and trained experts, all this is language that the simple answer is, you put Yes." Check that box with confidence, he says. Maybe you gave a talk to your local Chamber of Commerce or were involved in a simulation at your university with a former policymaker. Don't be shy about making claims for your ability to communicate your findings. You've been doing it all along.

Matthew Jacobs, who works in the intelligence community, notes that his PhD work and his teaching trained him "to go through different sources and distill the information into a digestible format, and that kind of language catches the eyes of these recruiters." A big part of an intelligence job is being able to take criticism, "so when you are able to say in an interview, hey, I've spent the last several years taking punches to the face on my papers from my advisers, I can handle that. I can take that email with comments, and I can take those comments on to make this a better paper."

Nonacademic writing can help too, even if many faculty members discourage students from writing op-eds, blog posts, and policy reports. After all, those don't do much to advance your academic career, which depends on peer-reviewed scholarship. But Kori Schake notes that a good op-ed can be great practice for making succinct, substantive arguments based on the empirical research you've done. This can get your broader work noticed and can help you learn how to communicate your ideas better than many academic articles do. "What I think is good about writing op-eds," she says, "is that they have a policy problem and an argument about what the answer is, and you have 700 words or less to say what you think should be done. Bad op-eds are just argument; great op-eds draw on data. . . . Established people can be lazy and rely on their existing credibility to get published; up-and-coming people actually have to be good at this to get published. So it's a good teaching tool."

Schake's caution about not relying just on argument but also on data is worth pausing over: your comparative advantage in proposing policy ideas comes not from powerful rhetoric but from your substantive expertise. Bold declaratory arguments that rely on straw-man tactics or breeze past complications may get attention, but they won't necessarily win you respect within the policy community. So if you want to write op-eds as preparation for your job hunt, go ahead—just make sure they show off your insights and judgment more than your command of language. As Kristin Lord notes, "Most people who have PhDs who go on to do other things, do it on the basis of being an expert in a definable area. They are a China expert, or they are an international development expert, or they are a defense expert—they are something. So, I think, often, it's a matter of leading with expertise."

Networking and Interpersonal Skills

You already know that networking is important when you are looking for academic jobs. That's why you presented at conferences while you were a graduate student. When you went to those conferences, you tried to meet as many people as you could. We've talked about programs (some policy focused, some methods focused) that can help build your networks and skills while in graduate school.

You can increase your networks in academia with help from your advisers. Especially if you are getting your degree at a major research institution, odds are that the faculty in your program know the faculty where you are applying for jobs, can help you get on conference panels, or can give you the opportunity to engage intellectually with senior scholars who visit campus. But those same faculty are not likely to be as equipped to help you create networks in the policy community. We've talked about how you can help yourself by attending a program like the Clements Center Summer Seminar on History and

Statecraft—those are the kinds of opportunities that not only help you connect with other students with similar interests but also enable you to get to know members of the policy community who come to speak and stick around for receptions and meals (or hikes, in the case of the Clements Center summer program, which is located in Beaver Creek).

What are other ways you can build your networks? Kori Schake did many interviews with current and former policymakers for her dissertation, so she met many people that way. In addition to interviews in the United States, she says, "I went to Germany and did some research and studied German, did a bunch of interviews in Germany which was also great fun, and then subsequently helpful when I went to [the Pentagon's] Joint Staff because I knew people all over the German military." You will not only meet people as part of your dissertation research but can also potentially go back to those people later to do informational interviews when you are starting to look for jobs. Steve Galpern advises students not to neglect the more obvious job-networking tools when looking for connections in a workplace that intrigues you: "Unlike in my time, there's so many more tools available to grad students now for making those connections, LinkedIn being a really big one."

Writing a dissertation can sometimes feel lonely or isolating; for pursuing a policy career, you are going to have to brush up on your social skills and get out there. Alice Hunt Friend lays out what you need to be able to do: "You cannot hide in your office. What is both necessary and sufficient is networking, and you build your social network with your social skills. So, you have to learn to make friends. You have to learn to remember names and faces. You have to learn how to be a good colleague." Galpern notes that being a good colleague can make or break your future opportunities: "All of the things you do in your job, you make these connections. And if you do your job effectively, people will notice you and remember you, and you will develop a positive corridor reputation, which is also very easy to trash if you don't behave well. . . . You will encounter people repeatedly in your career. It's amazing how much you do. So, if you're not going to be a decent person because it's the right thing to do, for goodness' sake, out of self-interest, be a decent person."

Friend also highlights a key dimension of working within any large organization or ecosystem full of people: understanding relationships and building trust. She advises, "You have to learn how to read the social cartography of policymaking. You need to know who's up and who's down. You need to know which friends not only have power today but will have power tomorrow, which feels really icky, but what I always tell young folks is, honestly, if you intend to last in Washington, just go make friends with the like-minded people you enjoy and just know that they're also going to be your colleagues and so, it's going to be kind of a strange friendship. But, over time, those are the people you will hire and who will hire you. They are the people you will call to ask, 'Should I hire so and so.' And I think the number one social skill, beyond just sort of making friends, is learning how to make people trust you and actually being trustworthy. That is your number one currency. And if you break trust with people enough, that will get around and that will create a serious ceiling to your career." Kori Schake agrees: "I have never had anyone who hired me for an important job do it on the basis of my published work. They have always done it on recommendations from people who know my published work. If you can cultivate a couple of people who know your work and are willing to be your advocates, that made all the difference in my career."

Earlier in this chapter, we mentioned the Future Strategy Forum that Sara Plana cofounded with a graduate student colleague of hers, promoting the ideas and work of women in the national security community. She notes that while networking wasn't her purpose in starting the project, "I've also been able to expand my policy networks among women, which has been especially important to me, and has hopefully helped other women do the same and that has been a complete boon to my career and my research, A lot of the leads I was able to get from my research came from that network, in particular, which was incredible and unexpected."

Reuben Brigety says that it's not enough to be a relationship manager if you want to achieve senior roles: "I mean, frankly, having particular policy expertise is very important for being a successful practitioner, but it's nothing close to what is ultimately needed. The real coin of the realm is when you combine policy expertise with leadership expertise. And I've seen a pretty big lacuna from interns that I've had, from seeing students, junior [Foreign Service] officers, who knew an awful lot about whatever particular country or region or issue but had minimal leadership or group organizational skills. The presumption is, you don't need them when you're younger, because eventually, when you become an ambassador or a DAS [deputy assistant secretary], whatever, you go to some kind of training institute and get them on the way; but actually, that is not my experience."

We've focused our attention on the Washington policy community, which is its own ecosystem. The private sector is often more dynamic, less insular, and more open to "cold calls," based on a declaration of shared interest. You can pursue these opportunities on your own initiative, without needing much help from others. Jennifer McArdle says of the start-up world that "if you're working on a problem that a start-up cares about, then it's just about reaching out to them and expressing interest in the company and their mission. Start-ups are constantly looking to hire people, and they're often willing to create jobs if you're interesting to them and can demonstrate how your expertise or experiences will serve their mission. Once you get into a start-up, if you have a unique background where you have a continued public presence through policy publications or speaking engagements, you'll get headhunted. You don't have to look for your next job."

Working out in Silicon Valley, Paul McLachlan reminds us that the hiring process in his world is very different from the academic job market. There are huge numbers of openings, and he advises people to look well beyond the small number of companies that all of us have heard of, particularly since in his view, "there is incredible and meaningful work happening in both big tech giants and smaller start-ups. I think that the biggest difference is just thinking of hiring happening all the time." You don't have to wait until the job market opens in the fall or at an annual conference. In Silicon Valley, it's happening right now.

Even though the private sector may be easier to break into than the policy community or academia, anything you can do to find mentors will benefit you, no matter where you end up. And don't forget to pay it forward later, when you are in a position to mentor those coming up behind you.

Be Flexible

If you've applied for any academic jobs, you've been asked to state your research agenda. You're expected to have one that is well defined and is relevant to the academic field you're in. By contrast, in policy, you will not go far by declaring your intent to focus on a narrow zone of expertise. Flexibility in the policy world is critical. You can't go into an interview or a job with the idea that you have one area of expertise and you aren't comfortable outside that. Unless you are at a think tank (and even there, perhaps not until you are more senior), you'll be asked to work on someone else's project, not yours. You want to focus on the skills you've developed and what you can contribute to the larger effort—not your specific research puzzle. Wesley Reisser reflects, "You need to come into a career in policy ready to be flexible and move in other directions than necessarily where you first landed. So, like for me, a border expert, my first job after the PhD was on that. I haven't been working in that exact space ever since. Maybe someday I'll find my way back there but that just hasn't been where I've been since, and that's OK."

Erin Simpson helped build a successful defense consulting business, in part through her skill at talent spotting. She advises, "The last thing I tend to look for, and you can't really tell this from a résumé, so it has to come out in conversation, is how tied is the person to their research agenda? What I tell them is you study what I ask you to study, and that either totally bristles you, or you're like, sweet, I can do that." She notes that those joining the policy world after getting a PhD have to be comfortable with looking for an entry-level position and joining a team.

While your dissertation years may have kept you tightly focused, your doctoral training is actually designed for flexibility: it gave you analytic tools and substantive knowledge that you can apply to a wide range of issues, countries, and challenges. Part of preparing for a policy job search is rediscovering and leaning into the intellectual curiosity and range that, we imagine, helped drive you into graduate school in the first place. Many of the people we spoke with for this book didn't have a clear idea of what they were going to do when they started their PhD; and even if they did, their ideas changed over time.

And many cite the role of serendipity, or unexpected opportunities to stretch in new directions, as main contributors to their career satisfaction. Steve Galpern, who leads an office in the Bureau of Intelligence and Research, notes, "I've never fixed on anything, and I think the reason I've enjoyed my career so much is I'm open to any opportunities. I generally try to find a place where I'm very happy, very fulfilled, intellectually and personally. But if something interesting comes along, I will always consider it."

Galpern realized after a few years that his chosen career at the State Department wasn't working for him: "I thought I was going to work at State's Office of the Historian for like forty years, and then retire, because it was a great job, and I initially really loved the work. And then I wound up publishing two volumes, and then, after the second volume, I couldn't imagine going through that process over and over again, even though aspects of the work were super interesting, and the work of the Office is critically important to the Department—and to the country, frankly. . . . What I didn't love was basically doing what amounted to the research for a dissertation without being able to say anything substantive about what I had done—that is, without sacrificing a lot of time outside of business hours to work on journal articles or conference papers, and certainly not a monograph. I should also note that a management crisis in the office at the time accelerated my timetable to leave." He wound up making a lateral shift within the State Department to the Bureau of Intelligence and Research; from there, he has had opportunities to work at the National Intelligence Council and on the National Security Council staff at the White House.

Your Work/Life Balance

We hope we've made clear by now that there is no single pathway to success. But you do need to make choices that are right for you, particularly when it comes to your work/life balance. Academia isn't easy. If you are on the tenure track, you are going to feel enormous pressure to publish in top peer-reviewed journals and with academic presses, even while you are also teaching and grading and doing university service. Those jobs tend not to have boundaries. But they are often flexible, and you can be home for dinner (unless you end up teaching in the evenings), and you can drop off the kids (and pick them up) at day care. You may have summers free to travel or do research. There is built-in flexibility, so even if you do end up working on nights and weekends around the family schedule, you can often do it from home.

If you have a policy job, especially if you are working in a classified environment, you usually can't take the work home with you. That might be nice once you are home, but you've got to be able to leave the office. Working in government, and in the Washington policy world more generally, one's schedule is largely dictated by the needs of one's principal officer, by the calendar of world events, or by the crisis of the moment in your portfolio. Dafna Rand has worked various jobs in government as well as at an NGO while raising three young children. She says, "I've worked really hard. A lot of my colleagues [from the Obama administration] left government and somehow found jobs that had easier hours. I did not. Being an executive at Mercy Corps was a lot harder than being on the National Security Council in some ways. It was hard to leave my kids to spend a week in Ethiopia or Guatemala, but the kids saw that I was trying to help communities at need, and I hope that dedication to service will stay with them."

Even if you are pursuing academic jobs, you may make choices about the kinds of jobs you are going to pursue based on what kind of research and teaching you want to do. Sara Plana told us that when she was on the academic job market, she applied "primarily to policy schools and to professional military education institutions; and that was a personal decision I made about the kind of research I want to do and the kinds of populations that, if I continue to teach, I would love to teach. I would love to contribute and serve in a policy job at some point. The questions are, what does that look like, and what sorts of pathways can I [take to] get there, while also building a career where I could support myself and my family." After we spoke with her, she went back into government in June 2022, working at the Pentagon.

Some of those we interviewed sacrificed a lot to work in conflict zones like Iraq and Afghanistan. Mara Revkin says of her time in Iraq that it was "years of fieldwork and time away from my family, and there's also an emotional toll. There is a cost to this that cannot be compensated." This work can have a high impact and can be meaningful—but it demands self-awareness and self-care. And for some, like Wesley Reisser and Steve Galpern, coming to Washington for a policy job was an attractive choice for personal reasons. Galpern and his wife wanted a place where they could both be professionally happy; Reisser wanted a vibrant gay community.

If you are choosing a policy career because you've recognized things about applied work that appeal to you or make good use of your talents (as we discussed in chapter 3), then recognize that your policy career need not look like anyone else's. It can and should reflect your values, your needs, and your choices. The goal of the advice given in this book is to help you recognize how your own passions relate to a policy career and to help you position yourself so that you have the best opportunities to make those choices that are right for you.

Sara Plana advises keeping a journal for yourself to record "what's important to me, and revisit that over time. It is OK if that changes; but it's important to be very deliberate about why it is changing. Is it because I have more information than I had before? Is it because I actually enjoy this more? Or is it socialization, is it because of other sorts of incentives? Just keep checking in with yourself that everything you're doing is because you want to be doing it. . . . It's easy to get sucked into the incentive structure."

And then there's the fact that failure is endemic to all careers, which may be hard for people who've only known success in school. Failure is certainly endemic in academia. Whether you are applying for jobs, applying for grants, or submitting your manuscripts to journals, you are going to fail far more than you are going to succeed, and that remains true throughout your career. In Silicon Valley, people try and fail all the time. Venture capitalists still look to fund new ideas, hoping for the next big thing, even if most of those ideas fail. Those who fail in the tech world don't have any trouble getting hired somewhere else. (That also seems to be the case for college football coaches.)

What's important is how you deal with failure. Mara Revkin notes that "academics experience a lot of failure but are only rewarded for success; in applied work, analyzing 'failures' is valuable; you learn from failure to improve policy and programs." Kori Schake reflects, "I am struck at the number of people I mentor who make choices much too safe for their talents and prospects because they are afraid of making mistakes. . . . They feel like you only get one opportunity and if you don't make a straight-line choice, or if you falter or are found to be deficient in some way you didn't recognize you needed to be successful at that, there will be no way to claw your way back and be successful. And I'm living proof that's not true. It's just not true." That's where a great mentor like Schake can help guide you.

It's OK to fail in any field. Learn from it. Just as you want to learn from the reviews sent to you by a journal where your paper has been rejected, you want to learn from any failures as you move on in your career. Kori Schake tells aspiring policy wonks not to be risk averse in the attempt to avoid failure; instead, she counsels, it's important to dive into the unfamiliar and to trust in your ability to learn from and overcome failure. "People who are afraid to be wrong, or are afraid that the consequences are going to be damaging, shouldn't be in the policy world, because you're going to be wrong. Ted Williams hit four balls out of ten. . . . The spray pattern of infield hits is what you're going for, and people can be wrong about a lot of stuff and still have pretty good policy because they're in the ballpark."

"You're wrong, and you dust yourself off, and you try to attenuate the problems you were wrong about," Schake continues. "Figure out the outcomes you don't want. A lot of policy work is foreclosing the worst outcomes."

Note

1. On note-taking and other skills, see Laila Sorurbakhsh, "Translating Social Science Skill Sets for Careers beyond Academia," *Practicing Anthropology*, Summer 2022, https://doi.org/10.17730/0888-4552.44.3.48.

6

Career Pathways in Foreign Policy

If you went to graduate school without a clear idea of what you would do with your PhD, or if your initial plan evolved or just didn't pan out, you are not alone. And if you are still thinking about your future and aren't sure how to envision the career you want—well, you aren't alone either.

In the preceding chapters, we've tried to demystify the foreign policy world and illuminate what different types of policy jobs look like. We've shown you how to think about which types of jobs might make you happy, how to prepare yourself for the policy job search, and how to present your skills and expertise to potential employers. But can you envision a full career in foreign policy, given how wide and varied the policy ecosystem is? To help you do this, in this chapter we've assembled the voices and stories of policy professionals at different ages and stages of their professional lives. What you'll hear from them is that there is no single right path to a meaningful policy career. Many of them say their interests shifted over time. Many say that relationships with peers or mentors put new opportunities before them. And in many cases, career outcomes that they value highly were the result of serendipity. One common theme that emerges from these stories is that there is rarely a single make-or-break moment in a long policy career. Instead, there is plenty of opportunity to recover from setbacks and failures, to reinvent one's interests and goals, and to forge new roads to make a difference in a way that works for you.

Turning toward Policy

The former *Wall Street Journal* and *New York Times* journalist Carla Anne Robbins recalls, "At some point in my senior year in college, my mother said to me, 'What are you going to do?' And honestly, and truly, I had never thought about it. I didn't really have an idea. So I applied to graduate school, because the one thing I knew how to do was go to school." Similarly, Mara Revkin reflects, "At the beginning, I loved research. I thought I was convinced I could be happy just spending five years doing a lot of research without worrying too much about what I would do next."

The chance to get a graduate degree without taking on more debt has become an increasingly significant motivating force in recent years as the costs of college and other graduate school paths have skyrocketed. Sara Plana knew she wanted to work on defense policy after graduating from college. She hadn't thought about doing a PhD until her master's thesis adviser suggested it to her, but she figured she couldn't afford it. And then her adviser informed her that PhD programs are often funded. She started working at the Department of Defense, but her adviser had planted the idea in her head that she should consider getting a PhD. So she did pursue one, knowing that if she did, she would be able to return to a policy role or be able to inform policy from outside.

Once you are enrolled in a doctoral program, however, it's hard to avoid the pull from peers and faculty to focus on a tenure-track faculty career. The economist Erik Durbin wasn't too sure of his career goals when he started his PhD program, but he says he fairly quickly understood that becoming an academic was clearly the first choice for faculty and students in his program. He applied to nonacademic positions when he finished his degree, but like his classmates, he saw those as "fall-back positions." He started his career as an assistant professor at Washington University in Saint Louis but says, "I was starting to doubt how much influence I would have on the world as an academic. And so, that made me want to move to DC and to be more involved in policy, do work where I was interacting with people more as part of my day-to-day work life. I enjoyed teaching, but teaching was not valued that much in that job. The thing people really cared about was publishing, and that was becoming less and less interesting to me."

Mara Revkin says, "My first opportunity with the UN came out of exploratory field research in southeastern Turkey interviewing Syrians about their experiences living in Islamic State–controlled areas after my first year of coursework, which resulted in a *Foreign Affairs* article that was then read by someone with the UN who happened to be looking for an academic to conduct related research. They were looking for a more senior scholar, but they couldn't find one, so I was very lucky they emailed me out of the blue. That first project led to more opportunities with the UN that I was able to integrate with my dissertation research." After consulting for the UN, Revkin has now pivoted to a faculty position; she started as an associate professor at the Duke University School of Law in July 2022.

We've discussed how to start thinking strategically about building your skill set, your networks, and your opportunities while you are in your PhD program. And even then, there's a lot of luck involved. As Ivo Daalder notes, you can't go into a PhD program thinking you're going to be a senior fellow at the Brookings Institution because there aren't that many positions at Brookings to step into. "It's not going to happen unless you're lucky." But there are lots of ways to make luck for yourself and move into a career where you can make a difference, even if it's not what you envisioned when you set out.

Box 6.1. Profile: Bringing Social Science to the Defense Industry

Erin Simpson, senior adviser in industrial base policy at the US Department of Defense and former director, strategy development and deployment, space systems, at Northrop Grumman.

Erin Simpson graduated from high school in 1997 and from the University of Kansas in 2001. She began thinking about a PhD in political science in her junior year, thanks to excellent mentors like professors Phil Schrodt and Deborah "Misty" Gerner. Working as a research assistant for them, she was able to connect with Jon Pevehouse, who was in graduate school in political science at Ohio State and had been a couple of years ahead of her at Kansas, where he also worked as a research assistant for Schrodt and Gerner. Pevehouse explained to her that PhD programs are usually funded, which was not the case for law school, the other idea she had about her future. "At the time," she says, "I wanted to be a professor. I was very into the quantitative and statistical pieces that modern political science was offering. I wanted to be a professor in the Big Ten when I finished" (as Pevehouse would go on to do, at the University of Wisconsin).

But then history stepped in: Simpson started graduate school in the government department at Harvard University on September 12, 2001, the day after the terrorist attacks on the United States. She still thought she would go on to an academic career, but by 2004–5, she started having doubts. She was working on intelligence and information availability and counterinsurgency campaigns. In the fall of 2006, she was sitting in a conference room where an academic job talk was about to take place, and her department chair sat down next to her. The chair asked what her dissertation was on, and Simpson told her it was on counterinsurgency campaigns. The chair asked her, "Counterinsurgency, does anyone really care about that?" At that moment, Simpson realized that academia might not be a good fit.

Simpson attended the Summer Workshop on the Analysis of Military Operations and Strategy in 2003, and two years later she spent the summer as a RAND summer associate. Through that program, she met senior defense policy leaders like John Nagl, David Kilcullen, and Janine Davidson. She talked with Al Stam, who was on her dissertation committee, about her nonacademic interests, and he was very supportive of her change in trajectory. In the spring of 2007, she moved home to work on her dissertation and then got a job at the Marine Command and Staff College at Quantico. She moved to DC a few months later and worked at Quantico for two years. She lost the job at Quantico because she hadn't finished her degree, and Davidson encouraged her to get the dissertation done. "Your only job," Davidson said, "is to submit." Simpson says she "finished the PhD out of spite. Nothing made me angrier than when other people suggested, 'Well you know, you don't have to finish this.'"

After she left Quantico, Simpson spent a year in Afghanistan as a counterinsurgency adviser, thanks to Kilcullen, who was putting together an advisory team at the request of General Stanley McChrystal. When she got back to Washington, she learned that Kilcullen was "building a company around this project that would do some kind of data science or edge processing to support the tactical warfighter." Simpson had statistics and data analytics from her graduate training, and so she joined the team as social science lead. The applied social science firm the team built, called Caerus, did conflict assessments in Syria and Afghanistan and a few projects with the World Bank. She reflects, "Having a really solid grounding in certain kinds of conflict dynamics and even basic research design was really helpful when we were designing assessments for USAID." Social science also gave her the necessary background for conducting surveys: "I could not have done this without the research skills and the specific conflict studies-type training that I got." And she reflects on how proud she is of the people they hired, and what they went on to do after they left the firm, which, she notes, is analogous to how a professor feels about the students they train.

Simpson notes that the direction she chose fit well with her personality. "I'm really good at making decisions," she says, "I'm actually really good at building teams. I like to spend my time pulling together information. I like to corral those resources and decision points to try to get people to a good kind of business outcome."

Simpson told us that the demands on her schedule, whether in government or outside it, were very different than they are for academics. When she worked at Northrup Grumman, it "really [owned] me more or less 8:00 AM to 6:00 PM, Monday through Friday." But, she added, on the flip side at Northrup Grumman, "They [didn't] want my weekends, almost ever, that's sort of by exception. I [didn't] work after six very often, unless [I was] doing something for the West Coast or something specific [came up]. They [were] my working hours, and the working hours [were] sort of set in a vaguely humane, or at least a semistructured way." Today, Simpson is back in the US government, working as senior adviser on industrial base policy at the Department of Defense.

You, too, may start graduate school thinking you want to be a professor when you finish, only to find out as you go along that you want to pursue a different path. Simpson found a path that suited her personality, her work style, and her interests. She did it by taking chances and finding great mentors.

If you know going into graduate school that you don't want to be a professor when you come out the other end of the program, then finding the right mentors is key. Having professors who encourage, rather than discourage, your interests is critical. As a former career diplomat, Stephen Del Rosso feels fortunate that, despite being older than his classmates and continuing to work in full-time jobs involving extensive travel after he left government, he had a dissertation supervisor, the University of Pennsylvania political scientist Ian Lustick, who was supportive of his interests and ambitions. Advisers like Lustick and Barry Posen, whom we met earlier in the book, may also be more willing to let you focus your writing on the issues that move you rather than what's considered de rigueur for your academic discipline. That might help you get through your program faster and happier, as it did for Kori Schake.

Box 6.2. Profile: Culture and Leadership, in and out of Government

Kori Schake, senior fellow and director of foreign and defense policy studies at the American Enterprise Institute.

"I have a question that threads through my professional life, which is a question of political culture: What makes some states aggressive, what makes some states wealthy, what makes some states stable?"

Sometimes the intellectual threads that run through our careers are visible only in retrospect; but if we are driven by the questions we find most compelling, those threads become clear over time. The investigation of culture, for Kori Schake, has extended beyond the domestic sources of foreign policy behavior to understanding the policy-making institutions of the US government. It led Schake to work within, and then write about, the Pentagon and the State Department; it has shaped her work on civil-military relations and her 2017 book on the transition from British to American hegemony.[1] Today, Schake puts her understanding of organizational and political culture to work leading a team of nearly fifty people in the Foreign and Defense Policy Studies Division of the American Enterprise Institute, a storied conservative think tank that was home to Ambassador Jeane Kirkpatrick, among others.

Like many of the other policy professionals you are meeting in this book, Schake did not embark on her graduate education with a clear vision for her career trajectory. She relates, "I was a reasonably smart, dreamy kid who didn't have a plan, got to the end of college and thought I could stay in school because I didn't have a better plan, and it was validating. So I'm the worst example of doing a PhD." As we now know, she isn't the only one!

Schake found her path, she says, thanks to mentors in undergraduate and graduate school. Her Stanford professor, Condoleezza Rice, hired her to research personnel policies of the Soviet and American militaries. "I was doing research for a book she never ended up writing and that was the professional making of me," Schake laughs. Winning admission to the University of Maryland's doctoral program in government and politics introduced Schake to professors like Catherine Kelleher, founder of Women in International Security, and the famed strategist Thomas Schelling. These mentors, Schake says, saw her interest in applied work and directed her to courses, fellowships, and other opportunities that would help her nurture and advance her in a policy career: "They saw my strengths and weaknesses and consciously pushed me toward work [that] they could see my eyes lit up in the doing of it; ... all three of those early mentors were all people who did applied work."

Looking back, Schake knows that this way of doing her graduate work effectively closed the door on a tenured academic role. But she found a career path that better suited her interests. With the encouragement and support of her graduate school mentors, Schake applied for, and received, a fellowship from the American Association for the Advancement of Science (AAAS) to work within the US government. Her part-time boss at that moment was a retired general, who suggested she take the AAAS fellowship to the Joint Staff so that she could build expertise in military affairs. Schake ultimately spent six years at the Pentagon, while she was still all but dissertation at the University of Maryland.

The end of the Cold War helped drive Schake's interest in joining the government. She notes, "I'm a European expert and so much was changing and so the chance to try, even in a small way, to influence the course of events that had felt frozen in time for some time, and now were in motion. . . . It was mostly a sense of excitement with the problems and that this is going to be so much fun. So I'd like to say I was noble and civic-minded, mostly that's not true. It was mostly, 'This is going to be so much fun.'"

After leaving the Defense Department, Schake spent time as a fellow at universities on both coasts, and she then joined the George W. Bush administration on the National Security Council staff, working for her former professor from Stanford, Condoleezza Rice. She took a brief break from government to teach at West Point and then returned for a tour in a third component of the executive branch's national security apparatus, the State Department. She was the deputy director of the Policy Planning Staff, a team of analysts who undertake projects directly for the secretary of state (and an office that is quite amenable to academic-type thinking). She left the department to become John McCain's foreign policy adviser during his 2008 bid for the presidency; she also wrote a book for the Hoover Institution comparing the organizational cultures of the Pentagon and the State Department to illustrate how the latter organization could improve its policy impact through more attention to training, leadership, and mining past experiences to shape future efforts.

Schake is recognized today as not only a leading conservative policy thinker on national security but also as a skilled leader of policy professionals. She has held senior executive roles at the State Department and at two different national security think tanks—the International Institute for Strategic Studies in London and the American Enterprise Institute in Washington. And her life lessons about taking risks and making "51–49 policy decisions" frame her approach to leadership. She says the most enjoyable part of leading a team of policy scholars is "pushing people to ask actually interesting questions. It is striking how much incredibly talented people want to do what they're already good at, or want to ask the same question over and over, . . . making people feel safe and trusted enough that this is interesting and important work, . . . making it safe to be wrong, and being wrong for long periods of time, because Edison produced 1,000 light bulbs that didn't work before he got one that did."

We tend to think of pursuing a PhD as a full-time endeavor, and it certainly requires less juggling if that's how one goes into a program. But Schake isn't the only person we spoke with who did a PhD while also working full time in another job. If one has a family, the added responsibilities of pursuing a PhD can create strains at home, as Stephen Del Rosso learned while embarking on this path when he began working in philanthropy at the Pew Charitable Trusts and, later, while completing his dissertation during his initial years at the Carnegie Corporation. But it can also be a way to ensure that you remain focused on your purpose in doing the PhD, if that purpose is not to get a tenure-track job. Combining work and doctoral study also may not be zero-sum, as Wesley Reisser found out.

Box 6.3. Profile: A Geographer Breaking New Ground

Wesley Reisser, deputy director of the Office of Human Rights and Humanitarian Affairs in the Bureau of International Organizations at the US Department of State.

Wesley Reisser has spent nearly twenty years in the State Department as a civil servant, but beyond that one stable fact, his career has brought him delightfully unexpected work. He began working at the State Department even before finishing his undergraduate degree at George Washington University, and he completed his master's in geography part time while working as a consular officer and then a desk officer in the Israeli and Palestinian Affairs Office in the State Department's Near East Bureau. His background in human geography—the relationships between places and people, including borders and political and cultural history—enabled him to contribute unique insights to the final status negotiations then under way between Israelis and Palestinians as part of the Annapolis Peace Process led by Secretary of State Condoleezza Rice. Geographers, he says, "work on the exact same set of issues as a political scientist or an economist or a historian that also might be competing for these same jobs. The difference is you think about things in a different way. You think about them spatially first, think about the relationships between places, and that can involve all kinds of questions like distance, region, and resources, and how borders have changed over time and the overlay of different ethnic groups and religious groups within a specific place."

With this opportunity for policy engagement and impact, why leave to pursue a doctoral degree? Reisser says his master's adviser "really pushed me to go on for a PhD. And at the time, I was kind of fed up with State and ready to leave." At the same time, he notes, "I looked at school as the time to take classes that would be interesting to me, things that would help me grow and think about the world in different ways."

A senior colleague of Reisser's encouraged him to keep the option of government service open; it turned out that he could remain active in the Civil Service during his doctoral program by transferring to the Los Angeles Passport Agency and working there two days a week during his PhD studies at UCLA. When he finished coursework and examinations, his personal priorities led him back to his old job at the State Department, where he wrote his dissertation at night. "Why did I stay at State? . . . There were no [academic] jobs I wanted to take. The academic job market in geography in the United States is pretty limited, mostly land grant universities, and the jobs that were open in my subdiscipline were all in small towns; . . . as a young gay guy, the last thing I wanted to do was move to a tiny town in Kansas, whereas I could stay in Washington in a vibrant city."

When the Israeli-Palestinian negotiations stalled in 2010, Reisser turned his talents to a global agenda, working on American policy toward human rights, conflicts, and other issues at the United Nations. In his role at the International Organizations Bureau, Reisser has been able to use his academic expertise in a new way: "In the system I work in now, what we have to do is get more countries to side with us than against us, and a lot of that was done in a very ad hoc fashion. . . . I can bring a lot of longer-term historical memory as well as a lot of geopolitical theory to look at how blocs [of countries] are aligning now versus the past and help us map out what we call within the UN space, the 'movable middle,' states that exist somewhere between the United States and its close like-minded partners, and our adversaries. . . . Being able to bring this geopolitical analysis and look for ways to build commonality with those states that are in the middle is how you navigate the system to get big things done." Reisser and his colleagues turned that framework into a statistical model that allows them to give the State Department's senior officials a more precise understanding of whether US-sponsored efforts are likely to garner sufficient votes to succeed in UN bodies: "When the US runs for election, like for the Human Rights Council, we can't go to the president and say 'We have a gut feeling that we're going to win.'"

Reisser is proudest of his impact on US policy when it comes to advocating for LGBTQ+ rights. This mingling of the personal and professional has been a moving and unexpected dimension of his career. A few years before Reisser joined the State Department in 2003, being homosexual was still seen as an automatic security risk and a legitimate basis for the government to deny or revoke one's security clearance. "I came in [to the Department] not even knowing, will I tell the people in my office. So the idea that only eight years later it would be an actual, listed part of my portfolio of work is in and of itself kind of head-spinning to me. . . . I never saw myself as an activist. I went to college and I was planning to be some buttoned-up bureaucrat at the time, right, with the suit and tie, by doing whatever it is that they do. It never occurred to me that I was going to be working in those kinds of spaces someday down the road."

Finding Mentors and Sponsors

Mentors can be professors, as was the case for Kori Schake (who benefited from academic mentors with significant experience in policy), or they can be practitioners, as they were for Erin Simpson. But everyone needs help along the way, especially as your work takes you into new issue areas or regions. "The people who have helped me navigate my career at State," Wesley Reisser says, "have been both folks from within State and then I would say also from civil society that work on some of the issues that I've worked on . . . ever since coming in to the human rights world, which is huge; it encompasses hundreds of thematic issues in every country on the planet. You need a great network beyond just your internal network to be successful in that kind of space and to navigate where you go next in that space. So my mentors definitely include current State Department people. They also include great people from the think tanks and NGOs and they also include people I worked with previously at the State Department who've left, including political appointees who've come and gone but are people I've managed to stay in touch with and have been really great touchstones on what to do next."

A good mentor isn't just someone who imparts their wisdom to you. A good mentor also listens to you, and what you want to do, and how you want to make a difference. They aren't helping you do what they want you to do; they are giving you guidance and steering you toward opportunities to help you do what you want to do. Of course, you may not know what you want to do, and that's OK. But think hard about how you like to work, what type of work is meaningful to you, and how you want to use your nonrecreational or nonfamily time. That will enable a good mentor to help you pursue a career path that's a good fit for you.

If You Go into Policy, Can You Go Back to Academia?

It's conventional wisdom that while you can start out in academia and then move into a policy or private-sector career (as people like Erik Durbin, Jennifer McArdle, and William Ruger have done), you can't do the reverse. The thinking is that faculty are suspicious of people who left the academy, or those people who weren't publishing academic books and articles while they were away, so they can't compete if they decide they want to apply for a faculty position at a university. As Erik Durbin points out, "When I finished my PhD, I had the perception that if I start with an academic position, I have an option of going into policy, but the opposite might not be true, and I think that's probably still how people think about it. And it's hard to disentangle, like how much of that is signaling or something like that, and how much of that is once you go into a policy job, you're less likely to publish things, either because you don't have the time or because you don't have that incentive that the tenure clock gives you."

It's true that an extended period of time in the policy world is going to make it harder to get a tenure-line job in a political science, history, economics, or geography department. But those aren't the only academic jobs out there. More and more universities have launched policy schools or degree programs. These include master's degrees in public policy, public administration, and international affairs. These programs are designed to train students for the professional work-force. And thus while the faculty by and large (especially the tenured faculty) are career academics, there is a valued place for practitioners, especially those with PhDs and those whose professional networks can be of benefit to students and alumni. There's also the route Susanna Campbell chose: after launching a successful career in the policy world, she decided to get her PhD, received a postdoc in Geneva, and then took a tenure-track position at American University's School of International Service, where she was awarded tenure in 2022.

If you have a policy career, you likely won't have the peer-reviewed publications and other qualifications required to be hired later into a tenure-line position. But you might not care, particularly if the school treats its practitioners with respect and includes them in non-tenure decision-making in the program, such as decisions about the curriculum. (Some do, some don't—you should ask before you take such a position.) After Carla Anne Robbins left the *New York Times*, she took a position at CUNY's Baruch College for what she thought would be for one year. The leadership at the school wanted to create a master's in international affairs. Who better to write the proposal—fast—than a former journalist with a PhD? She did it, and they asked her to become the first director of the program. "I do help make academic decisions and I've been a longtime member of the curriculum committee. But this is a public policy school, very focused on real world research—and getting our students real world jobs—so this is also a lot like running a department at the *New York Times*," she says. And her role as a program director is a natural one for PhDs who have worked outside academia.

However, leaving the policy world to go to a full-time university-based position isn't the only way to connect with academia from the policy world. Teaching as an adjunct, as some of our interviewees like Jon Rosenwasser and Erin Simpson have done, and as many think tank scholars do, is probably the most common way for practitioners to maintain a foot in the academic world. Wesley Reisser published his dissertation as an academic book even as he invested in his State Department career. And in the intelligence community, it is common to find folks who regularly attend major academic conferences like the International Studies Association's annual meeting.

Those who are new to their careers, like Sara Plana, may try to hang on to both university and policy options as long as they can. She remarks, "One of my passions is research and my other passion is policy impact. And so, my career has always been, how do I feed both addictions." Then there are those who are further along in their careers, like Wesley Reisser, who says that he can qualify for early retirement in six years but would still be young enough to want to pursue other options, perhaps at a university: "I can come in as a professor of practice at that point. . . . I think that could be a really exciting model. I had some really great professors, especially at GW, who are professors of practice and they brought so much real-world experience plus deep academic knowledge into the classroom. And I think we need more of that."

Box 6.4. Profile: Taking the NGO Experience into Academia

Rebecca Wolfe, senior lecturer and executive director of international policy and development, Harris School of Public Policy at the University of Chicago.

"I was always interested in the intersection of psychology and political science," says Rebecca Wolfe. She interned at the Peace Research Institute Oslo between her junior and senior years of college, where she was introduced to the work of Harvard professor

Herbert Kelman. She called him up to say she wanted to work with him, and it turns out that it was his last year taking on new students. "I was always more interested in applied work, and wanted to study with Herb given his work with Israelis and Palestinians." She was less excited about the lab work in psychology, but she stuck with it; spent more and more time at the Kennedy, Business, and Law Schools; and then took a postdoctoral fellowship at Princeton University's School of Public and International Affairs. She applied for academic positions. "But still no one knew what to do with me, since my c.v. was sort of all over the place," she says. "I didn't have the traditional psychology studies, and then I often got bored every time I ran a lab study because everything was so pared down that it no longer looked like the phenomenon I cared about. And I was up for a job at the Wagner School of Public Service at NYU, and I basically said if I didn't get that job, I was leaving academia because I had so many resources at Princeton and I wasn't productive. I was getting to learn that this wasn't for me. I wanted to do applied conflict work, but I actually really didn't know what that meant." She had some experience in development as a work-study student at Partners in Health, working with Paul Farmer. To learn more about what an applied career would look like, the Princeton career services office helped her by setting her up with informational interviews.

A big challenge for many going the nonacademic route is that rather than deciding what you want to work on, you need to build a consensus within an organization. "You have less freedom to set your own research agenda," notes Wolfe. "When I moved back into a research role, that was one of the hardest parts for me. When I led the conflict unit at Mercy Corps, I got to set the research agenda as well, with collaboration from the research team, but then when I moved to the research team, the director of the conflict team wanted to direct it." And she thought, "I want to implement my vision. I don't want to implement your vision." She had joined Mercy Corps in 2006 to train staff in negotiation and to use social science theory to design peacebuilding programs. In 2010, they decided to start a research operation in 2010 and approached Wolfe to help initiate it. That first study led to a vibrant "youth-in-violence research stream."

What does she take away from having gotten a PhD? "It's being able to apply different frameworks to data and having that organize thinking. Really being able to think critically about the data. It's not just to run the regression, but actually understanding what it means. One of the hardest parts in a nonacademic role, on a team not full of academics," she says, is when your boss "doesn't know how to bring [those skills] out."

Over the years, despite not having gotten the job at Wagner, but living in New York City, she ended up mentoring students there. And she has now returned to academic life with a position at the Harris School of Public Policy at the University of Chicago. Having returned to academia after years working in the NGO world, she is not in a tenure-line position. But the students gravitate toward her because of her practical experience. "Most of my classes are still overrun," she notes, "and my office hours are busy."

She's also taken the time to write a piece on careers outside academia for PhDs. In it, she distinguishes between research jobs ("generators of knowledge") and nonresearch jobs ("consumers of knowledge"). She writes, "I spent the majority of my career at Mercy Corps designing peacebuilding programs. One of the reasons I believe I was successful is that I could bring in the evidence base and assure our donors that what we were proposing was grounded in what we knew." While a PhD was not required for the work she did, she writes, "I believe wholeheartedly that my success in my program design role, and later as director of the peace and conflict unit, was due to my PhD."[2]

As we have seen, Erik Durbin took a faculty position after completing his PhD, and he then decided to switch paths while on the tenure track. William Ruger left a tenured academic job at Texas State University to work at the Charles Koch Institute and the Charles Koch Foundation. Kristin Lord started her post-PhD career in academic administration, but she was keen to get policy experience: "One of the only intentional things I've ever set out to do in my entire career was to get a CFR International Affairs Fellowship. I could tell I had a fairly narrow view, and I just heard wonderful things about this. And I thought I would really like to get that, and it was safe. You had a job waiting for you when you came back, you could test it out, you can get a different perspective. It's kind of like going on an exchange program. And so I put together a panel, I set up a murder board for myself. It's the only time I've ever been organized about something in a proactive way about what I want to do in my career. And I did get it. And it was completely transformative." Matthew Jacobs went briefly into a teaching position while he was trying to land a government position, which he was able to take up a short time later.

Box 6.5. Profile: A Historian inside the Intelligence Community

Matthew Jacobs, briefer, President's Daily Brief Staff, Office of the Director of National Intelligence.

As an undergraduate, Matthew Jacobs became interested in the history of US foreign relations. During college, he also traveled abroad, working as a tennis coach in Switzerland. Given his burgeoning interest in the world, he decided to get a master's at the University of North Carolina, Wilmington. He became passionate about US foreign policy and found he liked being a teaching assistant and working with students, so he decided to pursue his PhD. In addition, his master's adviser, W. Taylor Fain, had worked as a Department of State historian before moving to Wilmington, so Jacobs didn't see academia and the policy world as distinct entities.

Jacobs chose to do his PhD at Ohio University under the direction of Chester Pach, drawn by the Contemporary History Institute that the historian John Lewis Gaddis founded and directed many years earlier. A fellowship from the institute allowed him to work on his dissertation elsewhere, so he moved to Charlotte, where his girlfriend (now wife) was living. Endeavoring to finish his dissertation but remain close to home, he took a job at a small Catholic high school just outside Charlotte. His adviser told him that it was fine to take the job but encouraged him to finish the dissertation, which he did. He then got a one-year position at Embry–Riddle Aeronautical University in Arizona. He was surrounded by academic practitioners who encouraged him to apply for government jobs. "I applied to 95 academic jobs," he says, "and I got three interviews. And then I got a positive hit from the government." Although he briefly took a tenure-track position at Anderson University in South Carolina, near his parents' home, he left after one year to take a job with the government.

Jacobs says a PhD is not a prerequisite to work in the intelligence community, but having one "shows this person has a deep intellectual curiosity. The key is how you present yourself, and that you're willing to say, I don't know everything, and I am willing to take on new ideas."

Jacobs has already had many opportunities within the community early in his career, serving at the time of this writing as a briefer on the presidential daily brief staff. How did he do it? He played up his ability to come up with material for teaching when asked to put together a class as a graduate student just before the semester started: "It was basically a rush job of me coming up with a class within two weeks with a syllabus, literally finishing lectures the morning before, and then going up in front of two hundred students and trying to act like I was an expert on the Han Dynasty. I said, 'I can work under pressure. I can work under tight deadlines. You can put me in front of people and not be worried that I'm going to embarrass you or the organization.'" He continues, "Being able to distill information, work under tight deadlines, get asked questions that you don't know the answer to, you don't want to get into the habit of just saying, 'I don't know.' You don't want to do that when you are in front of a roomful of nineteen-year-old students. You also don't want to do that on a regular basis in front of the director of national intelligence. You want to articulately give something, and at the same time say, but I can get you more on that. In my current position, I make a lot more phone calls to people. But just having that sense of, I need to go deeper on this issue."

Jacobs doesn't feel like he's turned his back on the academic community, and he hopes to teach again as an adjunct down the road.

In addition to having a boss and working as part of a team, the twists and turns in one's policy career path are perhaps the most dramatic difference from a traditional tenure-track academic position. The academic path, for those who are able to land a tenure-track position, is pretty well laid out. The requirements for being granted tenure at the end of your sixth year are usually quite transparent, even if the final decision-making can be opaque. Though some faculty members move from one university to another, many spend their whole career working their way up the tenure and promotion ladder at one institution. In other sectors, of course, moving from one job to another, and from one institution to another, is a normal part of a career path. The individuals we spoke with took advantage of opportunities and on many occasions took chances even if they didn't know where it would lead them. They weren't afraid to switch jobs, and even to switch sectors, if they found something they thought would interest them. And they leaned on their networks to bring them opportunities and to vouch for them for roles. And, sometimes, their experiences led them to make dramatic reevaluations of what they wanted.

Box 6.6. Profile: Leadership in Academia and in Government

Ambassador Reuben Brigety, US ambassador to the Republic of South Africa.

For Reuben Brigety, getting a doctorate after college was a step on a military career path he designed to emulate his role model, General Colin Powell. But the doctoral experience fundamentally changed his perspective and led him to a wholly unexpected way of working in foreign policy and national security.

Growing up in Jacksonville, Brigety was surrounded by a strong Navy community. So perhaps it's no surprise that he set his sights on a Navy career early on. "I had the whole GI Joe collection when I was a kid. Everything. Every action figure, every main battle tank, everything.... From the time I was 14, I did everything I could, and my life was structured to gain admission to Annapolis [the US Naval Academy in Maryland]."

But Brigety didn't just want to be a naval officer; he wanted "to be the Navy's answer to Colin Powell," who had served as deputy national security adviser, national security adviser, and then chairman of the Joint Chiefs of Staff. "So the plan is, I majored in political science in the Naval Academy. I knew, looking forward, that if I wanted to advise senior people like my heroes, like Admiral Crowe for example, that I needed to go get a PhD." Having won a scholarship, he headed off to Cambridge for graduate school.

"I go start my master's degree, and basically, I started to get asked questions from international students that were based on assumptions I didn't really know that I had: 'Reuben, you seem like a really nice guy, could you really launch a nuclear weapon if your country told you to do it?' Or talking with this young South African guy who walked with a permanent limp from a bullet he took from an Afrikaner police officer at Soweto when he was five. Or talking with friends who are Palestinians who have been pushed across a river. I mean, people who have been, real-world, subjected to policies of violence, all around the world, that were, as much as I had been preparing and thinking and studying about war, were not even part of my calculus."

When he returned to naval service, the challenges and contradictions that he confronted in Cambridge ate away at his mental health and, he says, "almost cost me my life twice." He realized that "as much as I love the Navy and the nation, I was not a warrior." He applied to the Navy to be discharged as a conscientious objector. His career plan, he notes, "was completely blown up. I mean, it wasn't even clear to me that I could even serve in the US government again." But after writing a dissertation on international humanitarian law and the use of cruise missiles in coercive diplomacy, he wanted to work on humanitarian issues in armed conflict. He found a job in the arms division of Human Rights Watch just before the September 11, 2001, terrorist attacks on the United States. "Within six months, I'm in Afghanistan for Human Rights Watch. I'm unarmed, undefended, doing some of the first human rights research missions of the war." Brigety sees his work on humanitarian affairs and conflict resolution as consistent with his early commitment to national service: "I love the United States of America. . . . I want to see this democratic experiment continue. And I know that, quite frankly, there is no scenario in which our interests or values are better served absent American leadership."

Brigety's career has taken him to leadership roles both in academia and in government. He taught international relations, first at American University and then at George Mason University, but dove back into public service via a Council on Foreign Relations International Affairs Fellowship that took him to the State Department. He was appointed by President Barack Obama to be the US ambassador to the African Union. After leaving that post, he served as dean of the Elliott School of International Affairs at George Washington University and then as the first Black vice chancellor and president in the history of the University of the South (Sewanee). In 2022, Brigety was confirmed to serve as US ambassador to the Republic of South Africa.

Brigety ascribes his success in both academia and government to the leadership skills he learned as a midshipman at the Naval Academy: "The lessons I learned there, I draw on daily." His personal journey, combined with those leadership skills and his religious faith, keep him firmly grounded and make him a formidable interlocutor for foreign counterparts. "I do know we live in a broader world. . . . And any American diplomat that has ever had to justify American foreign policy abroad always has the question

> of, 'yeah, but what about. . . . What about your CIA operations that are funding coups? What about your segregation and slavery at home?'. . . The beauty of America is that we are constantly interrogating the gap between our professed values and our lived experience, and trying to close the gap between the two. And the smaller that gap is, the more powerful we are, and I absolutely believe that."

There are also policy jobs that are more similar to the tenure-track path. While Ivo Daalder is correct that not everyone can become a senior fellow at the Brookings Institution, or at a similar think tank in Washington, there are those who do, like Tanvi Madan. And like professors at a university, there are many scholars who can build their whole career at one think tank, moving from fellow to senior fellow and perhaps founding and directing programs or centers, just like they would at a university. They may not be granted "tenure" or long-term contracts, but depending on the think tank, they may be able to stay on as a scholar as long as they remain productive (and, like some faculty, sometimes even longer!).

Box 6.7. Profile: An Academia-Adjacent Think Tank Career

Tanvi Madan, senior fellow and director of the India Project, Foreign Policy Program, at the Brookings Institution.

Does it make sense to pursue a foreign policy career if you never expect to work inside the US government? To Tanvi Madan, who was born and raised in India, the answer was a clear yes and led her to a career as a scholar at the Brookings Institution. Most foreign policy jobs in the US government require the employee to be a US citizen or, in rare cases, at least a permanent resident. Madan's work at Brookings is rooted in her expertise on two other international heavyweights, China and India, with which the United States has crucial and changing relationships.

Madan had long nurtured an interest in international affairs, in part because of growing up as the Cold War ended and the bipolar global order broke open, with major consequences for India. After college, she worked in the country's exploding tech sector while contemplating her options and applying to master's programs in both the United Kingdom and the United States. It was her experience at Yale's international affairs master's program that put her onto the policy path: "It was because of the people around me who had served in government and were thinking about going into a variety of foreign policy careers.... I was one of the younger folks there, I was twenty-three; government was not a career option for me at that point, but I discovered there were other foreign policy career pathways."

At the same time, the master's program and courses with Yale professor John Lewis Gaddis awakened Madan's interest in deeper research, especially diplomatic history and archival research: "Being able to do the research made me write better memos.... I liked the in-depth analysis, but I think it always helped to be able to step back and put it in a broader context." She further notes, "I wanted to contribute to knowledge that was going to be practical and not just in academia." She chose her doctoral program carefully, weighing political science (too quantitative), history (too uninterested in contemporary policy), and public policy programs. She ended up at the University of Texas at Austin's LBJ School of Public Policy. "It was a history professor who told me, 'You know, you can do the history stuff that you want to do [at Austin], because there are great historians at UT.'... If I went to the history program, at that time they would have seen any work I did on policy stuff as a distraction."

For Madan, pursuing a PhD was not just an opportunity to dive into research, develop issue expertise, and enhance her methodological rigor: "I also needed what one of my advisers called a hunting license, and as a young woman, the bar was higher to be taken seriously. To this day,... I have separate business cards for Asia that have my name, comma, PhD. Because it makes a difference." Madan relates how working at Brookings as a research assistant before her PhD program shaped her understanding and expectations, both positive and negative: the senior fellows were mostly older and men and white, but they nonetheless included scholars who became role models and mentors for her, like the India scholar Stephen Cohen and Jim Steinberg, who is now the dean of the Johns Hopkins University School of Advanced International Studies.

Madan emphasizes that think tanks vary widely in the level of academic training they demand from their researchers as well as in the length and depth of the research products they prefer. What all think tanks have in common, however, is a tight focus on influencing policy debates and policy outcomes. This, Madan says, puts a premium on scholars knowing their audience for a given piece of analysis and knowing how to pitch their argument correctly for that audience. In the Brookings Foreign Policy Program, she notes, the emphasis on sole-authored books makes a PhD very valuable. Madan observes that think tank scholars without doctoral training often struggle to structure and develop book-length work because they haven't practiced or developed that skill set. And especially for those without a PhD, she cautions, a book is an even more important marker of true expertise and a basis for one's reputation as an expert in a specific issue area.

Madan knows her choice to pursue a PhD in public policy likely closed the door to an academic career track, but for her the attraction of policy research is its unique combination of expertise and breadth of perspective: "I like thinking through, what is the landscape, who are the stakeholders, what are the options, anticipating the consequences.... You have to think about various agencies and corporations and foreign governments. You have to think about domestic politics. And to me, integrating all that ... was really interesting." She also takes satisfaction in bringing a broader array of younger scholars into the field, by reaching out to less-well-known universities when she travels within the US or elsewhere to give talks: "I had people who made it comfortable for me to do this weird thing that I was doing. And there are lots of other people, and I want them to feel comfortable too."

As we've emphasized throughout this book, the drive to make a meaningful difference is a key motivator for those who pursue a career in foreign policy. The stories given above have, we hope, given you inspiration as you reflect on what kind of impact you want to have in your own career. Before we conclude, in the next chapter we further explore what it means to make a difference working in foreign policy.

Notes

1. Kori N. Schake, *State of Disrepair: Fixing the Culture and Practices of the State Department* (Stanford, CA: Hoover Institution Press, 2012); Jim Mattis and Kori N. Schake, eds., *Warriors and Citizens: American Views of Our Military* (Stanford, CA: Hoover Institution Press, 2016); Kori N. Schake, *Safe Passage: The Transition from British to American Hegemony* (Cambridge, MA: Harvard University Press, 2017).

2. Rebecca Wolfe, "Considering a Non-academic Career: Some Musing from a Scholar-Practitioner," https://medium.com/@rebeccajaynewolfe/considering-a-non-academic-career-some-musing-from-a-scholar-practitioner-4856edd5df49.

7

Making a Difference Working in Foreign Policy

You can see from the examples and insights given in this book that foreign policy work encompasses a wide range of topical areas, working environments, skill sets, and personality types. The preceding chapters have given you ideas and models for foreign policy careers that might fit your passions and skills. We are confident that, if you want to work *in* foreign policy rather than *on* foreign policy, you will find a fulfilling place to put your talents to work.

Whatever the reason you picked up this book, we hope you can see clearly now that making your career outside the academy does not mean you failed to fulfill the purpose of your doctoral degree. Far from it. Foreign policy work is not a "second-best" professional option for social science PhD holders, but a demanding and rewarding career path in applied social science. It offers the opportunity to make meaningful impact on the world, on the people around you, and on questions related to, but quite different from, the questions that drive academic work in international affairs. In this final chapter, we focus on what makes working in foreign policy meaningful to the people who do it, and in what ways they feel able to make a difference through their work, just as academics feel able to make a difference in theirs.

If you become a university-based scholar, you will make your greatest impact through your research and teaching. People read your work, are better informed, and, in the case of public policy, might even make better decisions thanks to the careful and innovative work you have done. In the classroom, you will impart knowledge to your students and will help them develop critical thinking skills. If you are a scholar who wants to influence policy, your greatest impact might be not through what you write but through your ability to inspire students to go into public service, equipping them with the skills they need to succeed.

As we noted earlier in the book, some PhD holders are drawn to foreign policy over academic life because they want to shape policy directly rather than from a university research and teaching perch. Different career choices open different opportunities for impact. Working in policy instead of analyzing it from a distance also, unavoidably, engages the issue of power—how you respond to it and how you wield it. So we also cover some of the ethical issues you may confront in undertaking a policy career, and share advice from policy workers on how to stay true to the values and aspirations that drew you into policy in the first place.

A Community of Knowledge and Action

The policy world, like academia, offers PhDs an intellectual community—one that may be organized around shared subject-matter interests and may also comprise shared values, shared visions for change, and shared purpose. Tanvi Madan says that this community-building dimension of her work at Brookings is what she is most proud of in her career thus far: "Some of the things that I would love is when I was hosting a roundtable and I was introducing people who worked or were interested in India or Asia from different parts of the government that had never met each other before. . . . Yes, you get to brief high-level people. I still find it exciting that people who are in important positions think I have something useful to say, but to me it's really about the interesting people in this world."

Erin Simpson, whose scholarship in Harvard's government PhD program was focused on how to improve US counterinsurgency, felt isolated in her interests until she spent a summer at the RAND Corporation: "I discovered all these people who had been working on it. But I had just been in my library carrel. I had no idea there was a community in Washington that was diligently engaged."

Improving your piece of the policy community, fixing what you think is broken in the system, can also be a source of motivation and pride, as Jon Rosenwasser relates: "My joining [the Office of the Director of National Intelligence Staff and later the Senate Intelligence Committee staff] was driven by a desire to contribute to what I saw was the great public management challenge of our time—how to improve the management, operation, and oversight of intelligence in the wake of the erroneous assessments of Iraq's weapons of mass destruction program and the terrible terrorist attacks of 9/11. . . . Oversight of intelligence in a democratic society . . . [is] critical to intelligence durably and effectively contributing to our national security. Without it, there is substantial risk that intelligence runs amok and operates outside political norms and legal boundaries, becomes disconnected from the policies it is meant to support, and loses public support."

In building an intellectual community, wrestling with ideas, and perfecting your craft, a policy career can feed the same intellectual hunger that drove you into graduate school and that drives most academics. Steve Galpern finds this kind of fulfillment every day in his work as an intelligence analyst and manager: "Something one of my mentors imparted on me early in my INR [Bureau of Intelligence and Research] career, which I've found incredibly valuable, is that there are no wasted opportunities. Everything you write, even if it's a tree that fell in the woods, and you think nobody heard it, all of that is kind of building up your store of knowledge, it builds up your talking points, it builds up all these things that you know, so that next piece you write, or the ten pieces down the road that you write, are probably going to be a lot better for it, that much richer because you've done it, even if nobody read that piece. And when you brief, you're so much of a better briefer when you've written something, because the only way you actually know something, you've digested it, it becomes part of your DNA, is if you wrestle with the ideas and you write about it. . . . And so, I let people know that your time will come. If you're on an account long enough, your time will come." This doesn't mean the path is easy. Myriad obstacles can crop up along the way, including bad bosses who stymie your career path or budget cuts that send you looking for other jobs. Professional competition can be intense, and we hope that this book makes navigating this competition a little bit easier.

Playing a Team Sport

One theme that you've read a lot about already in this book is the degree to which foreign policy is a team sport. Indeed, the people we spoke with for this book emphasize how much of their impact and fulfillment come from their influence on others—teammates, colleagues, institutions, and principal decision-makers. Perhaps surprisingly, this seems to mean more to the policy workers we spoke with than their own development and marketing of policy ideas.

The ability to persuade allies, galvanize a consensus, and mobilize collective action (whether inside the bureaucracy or across time zones) typically does not flow from a "my way or the highway" approach. Dafna Rand explains it well: "You succeed again, and again, if you can give your ideas to others, and if you care about impact. If you want to change policy, the best way to do it is to work from the bottom up, give your ideas around gently and persuasively, and get other people to spread your ideas even if you are not in the room. Have people use [your] paradigm and perspective." She's right, but of course it can be frustrating for many people not to be in "the room where it happens," especially when it's your own ideas that are being discussed.[1]

For some policy professionals, the camaraderie of shared labor and shared sacrifice on behalf of a common goal is a deeply fulfilling part of the job. Jennifer McArdle enjoys knowing that her work helps people in the military do their jobs better; she also enjoys the collaborative and mutually supportive environment that endeavor generates: "Everything we create, I know someone within the defense establishment is going to use it—whether that is an intelligence analyst or a developer. . . . Feedback within our technology development process oftentimes feels more positive than feedback within academia. The military knows that we are trying to create tools to help them, so their feedback reflects that. Not everything we create is perfect, particularly on our first iteration, but we work iteratively and closely with defense users to refine our tools and make sure it meets their needs. The process overall feels like a more positive way of making mistakes and solving problems versus just being destroyed by reviewer number two."

Many of our interviewees also cite their work to mentor and nurture a rising generation of talent as a core component of what makes their work meaningful. Career academics are often known as much for the students they have taught and mentored as for their own published work. Our interview subjects working in foreign policy tell us that this intergenerational mentoring matters greatly to them too. This means that when you reach out to ask for advice from the PhD holders you admire in the policy world, you can expect to find a warm welcome.

Bending the Arc of Social Change

It is not surprising that many policy professionals come into the work from a long-standing commitment to public engagement and public service. They may have volunteered for humanitarian missions in high school, worked on political campaigns or issue advocacy in college, or, like many of those interviewed for this book, worked at a junior level in the US government before going to graduate school.

The economist Erik Durbin says, "I think I've been much more professionally satisfied with this path. . . . I think I miss some aspects of academia, but they're outweighed by the ability to be involved. To feel like I'm doing something to make a difference in the world is really important to me." You may likewise be drawn to policy work because you want to leave the world better than you found it: maybe you want to end wars, reduce human suffering, mitigate climate change, or expand human freedom. Obviously working in foreign policy is not the only way to change the world—but the power and reach of the United States mean that US foreign policy and the private sector have a profound impact in large and small ways all around the world.

Setting Aside the Purity of Positivism

In academic social science, we are encouraged to be "positivists"—to focus on provable claims and to abjure normative commitments that might bias our analysis. One significant difference in policy work is that the work, and the people undertaking it, are infused with normative premises, goals, and commitments.

In graduate school, students are typically trained away from speaking or writing in the first person when discussing US foreign policy.

They are trained to separate themselves from the actors they observe and analyze and to distinguish clearly between normative preferences and objective findings—extracting the former from their scholarly work to focus on the latter.

The Senate staff member Paul Bonicelli describes one moment when he confronted the gap between his commitment to making change and the academic positivism of his doctoral program in political science: "One girl I dated [in graduate school], she was totally academic. She didn't care about politics at all. And I was like, why are you interested if you don't care how it all turns out? The department was very quantitative, and I wasn't. I got a C in stats, and the chairman, who liked me a lot, was very quantitative, and he was very supportive of me. And he said, 'Look, there are a lot of us who are in this. We don't like to make any moral judgments. We want to look at the numbers and here's what the numbers say. You're different. You'd like to say this is how it should be.' And I said, 'You got that right!'"

Indeed, policy work can offer you an unparalleled opportunity to put your normative commitments into practice. Bonicelli adds, "The reason I'm so drawn to development and democracy is because I truly believe every human being should be free. They are created in God's image. . . . I fundamentally believe that I want every policy possible to reflect that and advance it. . . . You know, we can be very hopeless about development and all that. But we do know, there's pockets, there's people, there's success stories, they're there. And if that's all there is, that's fine. One person, it's worth it. I had a guy mock me one time, you know, 'Why do you want to support this micro-lending stuff, everywhere you go, it's a bunch of little poor ladies sitting at their little table next to each other doing the same thing.' And I said, 'You know why? The economics of it may not be what you want. But you know what her children see? Their mom was not begging anybody. You can't put a value on what that is for those children.'"

Even those in purely analytical roles, in places like the intelligence community or in think tanks, are operating in a context where their key audiences are actors with power and preferences. As an analyst, you must take account of those preferences to be effective, even when you avoid expressing preferences or making recommendations of your own. The intelligence community has developed strong norms and rules to ensure that it presents data-driven analysis without fear or favor, despite working for a client with the power to order the use of force. But we know from the experience of the Iraq War that intelligence work can be politicized, and even nonpartisan analysts can get caught up in the political fray. In his review of Robert Jervis's book on US intelligence failures in the Iranian Revolution and the 2003 Iraq War, the George Washington University political scientist James Lebovic observes, "The Bush administration, which tried to shift the blame to the IC [intelligence community] for the wrong judgment on Iraqi WMD [weapons of mass destruction], did question the IC's conclusions and make the IC work harder when it challenged the administration's judgments (e.g., on the link between Saddam Hussein and Al Qaeda). Other administrations have put substantial pressure on the IC to deliver analyses that affirm administration policies."[2]

Staying True to Your Moral Compass

The decision to use force is perhaps the most sobering example of the exercise of power in foreign policy. But choices with moral consequences abound in the foreign policy realm, and working within government, a company, or an NGO also means subsuming your personal preferences to the organizational imperatives, relinquishing a degree of autonomy in favor of collective impact. You have to get comfortable using the pronoun "we" and understanding that even when you lose internal debates about how to proceed, you are implicated in, and committed to executing on, the decisions that are made for your organization.

US government decisions are made by elected politicians and their appointed designees such as the secretaries of state and defense. Working in policy means living with that, and sometimes politics can be rough—reflecting egos and power and money more than ideas or logic. Bonicelli says, "Politics is fun to me. But it's never been the thing. It is a means to an end. I'm here now because my political friends put us together. I was working on other campaigns with people. And I don't diminish politics, I love it, I respect it, I'm always teaching students, if you disparage [it] and treat this as, it's just all dirty, [that's not right]. It's just how it works, it's how freedom works; . . . that's the way

I thought about it." Ultimately, working in the context of a democratic government means embracing that democratic legitimacy gives those politicians the right to make policy decisions—even when you think they are deciding things for the wrong reasons or in the wrong way. Reuben Brigety applies this view to the career services: "The people of the United States need a professional foreign policy corps . . . that will execute the orders and the perspectives of the government of the day, if we presume that democracy actually matters; . . . as a general proposition, you may find it more difficult to serve some governments that others. That, frankly, is one of the benefits of being a political appointee, because you're more likely than not going to be largely in tune with the orientation of the government you serve."

But, especially as one moves into more senior policy roles, whether in or outside government, the politics of a policy debate feature more heavily. Sometimes, as a policy official or advocate, you can see your policy concerns overshadowed by political considerations, and you might even find yourself personally caught up in the political controversy about a policy debate. Ideally, if that happens, it's because you made a conscious choice to take a stand rather than because you're someone else's convenient political football or fall guy. The advice given earlier in the book about setting ego aside for the sake of the mission applies here as well. Susan Rice—President Obama's campaign adviser, UN ambassador, and then national security adviser—says, "I think the people who do worst in this business are those that are really motivated by self. The self-interested people are the ones that either do something that's not helpful to the enterprise, and blow themselves up, or [who] are so sensitive to criticism that they either become an attacker or they just can't hang on, because it's all about them." (See box 7.1 for a special profile of Rice's experience navigating the heights of Washington's foreign policy architecture.) Reuben Brigety cites a dictum of Colin Powell's: "Never let your ego get so close to your position that, when your position goes, your ego goes with it."

Before embarking on a policy job, then, it's important for you to develop a conscious understanding of your own purpose, where your ethical boundaries lie, and what principles will keep you grounded in exercising whatever power you may have in the policy process. Brigety advises, "You need to figure out what your moral center, your theory of the universe is, and learn to trust it. Because, guaranteed, you are going to be someplace where you're not going to know which way is up and how to act when the stakes are high." He likens this moral centeredness to a lesson taught to scuba divers about what to do if you get spun around and disoriented while deep under water: "What they tell you to do is watch the bubbles, because the bubbles will always tell you which way is up. Where are your bubbles? What is your North Star? So, when things aren't right and you're disoriented, you can go to the bank on that. . . . You have to develop that capability before you need it."

Another question to ask is whether the institution you're looking at for work shares your values and appreciates the kind of impact you want to have. If so, you can probably happily put your professional ambitions in the service of the organization's mission. If not, you may well struggle to feel like your work is meaningful in the ways you crave. But it's rare to work in the policy world for long without confronting a gap "between our best values and our observed reality," says Brigety. "Government is not theology. We live in an imperfect world, and the question is, how do you constantly try to squeeze the gap? . . . and understanding where you think your limit is in that imperfection is important."

There are, of course, circumstances in which you might choose not to remain implicated by decisions you find odious—and that may mean resigning your policy role, speaking out publicly in ways that carry a professional price, or both. The late Jon Western, an accomplished professor of international relations and administrator at Mount Holyoke College, began his academic career after resigning from the State Department, along with three colleagues, in protest over the US government's failure to act to end the Serb genocide of Bosnian Muslims. Explaining his resignation in an interview with the *New York Times* in 1993, he said, "I found myself walking home every night just angry and bitter. My wife could tell you of my large mood swings. You can't read through the accounts of atrocities on a daily basis, add them up and see what's happening and not be overwhelmed. It calls into question your morality."[3] Brigety sums it up well: "Some things are more important than your position on an org chart." The former US government official and former Johns Hopkins School of

Advanced International Studies dean Eliot Cohen made this point in 2017, discussing whether anti-Trump Republican foreign policy experts should serve in that administration: "Public service means making accommodations, but everyone needs to understand that there is a point where crossing a line, even an arbitrary line, means, as Sir Thomas More says in *A Man for All Seasons*, letting go without hope of ever finding yourself again."[4]

Box 7.1. Profile: Reaching the Heights of Foreign Policy Leadership

Ambassador Susan Rice, assistant to the president for domestic policy and director of the Domestic Policy Council, White House; former assistant to the president for national security affairs.[5]

Susan Rice grew up in Washington, steeped in the city's political and policy debates that her father engaged in as an economist and her mother encountered as a trailblazing education policy advocate. Rice says she knew she'd need a terminal degree of some kind to do the policy work she was drawn to, and so after she won a Rhodes Scholarship, she stayed for a doctorate. But she insists that her PhD in international relations, while helpful, was not necessary for her career in public service. Her own experience drives the advice she gives to others who aspire to the heights of national security policymaking: to build a network that is as much political as it is professional.

For those who appreciate stability and consistency in a career, the Civil Service or Foreign Service can offer a path to senior policymaking. As Rice notes, however, "You can write the Foreign Service exam or join the intelligence community or go in via PMF or White House Fellow and hope somebody hires you. But that's an incredibly slow and uncertain path. And you're not likely to be in a position where you can rise anytime soon." If you want to reach a senior role more swiftly, she advises, "you have to be a political appointee." Rice knew her policy preferences aligned with the Democratic Party, and she volunteered for Michael Dukakis's presidential campaign in 1988, at the age of twenty-three. Dukakis lost to George H. W. Bush, and Rice pursued private-sector work at McKinsey & Company. But the relationships Rice forged with other Democratic policy hands meant that, when Bill Clinton won the presidency in 1992, she was offered the opportunity to join the new administration as a political appointee. She began on the National Security Council staff and was ultimately confirmed in 1997 as the assistant secretary of state for African affairs, the youngest person to serve at that level in a regional bureau at the State Department.

When the Clinton administration ended, a senior fellow role at the Brookings Institution offered Rice a chance to rebalance her family and work commitments as well as a platform from which she could "go global." Putting her experience on African issues into a wider context, and working with colleagues across Brookings, Rice broadened her issue set by publishing a landmark book on fragile states, conflict, and development. In 2007, she again made a political leap of faith: she chose to support Senator Barack Obama in his primary campaign against Hillary Clinton and took a full-time leave from Brookings to serve as one of Obama's senior foreign policy advisers. Obama's successful campaign landed Rice in the new administration, first as UN ambassador and then, in Obama's second term, as his national security adviser.

Active political engagement as part of a foreign policy career can, as Rice advises mentees, accelerate your career and take you to professional heights unreachable without political connections. It can also subject you to the harsh glare of political scrutiny and, not infrequently, political controversy that may have little to do with your actual job. Says Rice, "I don't know how you prepare for political attacks. I mean, the good news is you don't have to prepare for it in the early stages of one's career. You have time to get in there and get the experience and decide whether you have the appetite for it. Nothing prepares you like the rough and tumble of policymaking in Washington, except experiencing it. The higher you rise, the more knives there are, and that's not for everybody, obviously. Even when you have tolerated it to the extent that somebody like me has, it doesn't make it fun."

But the experience also sustained and strengthened Rice's commitment to making a difference through government service, even after a bruising eight years in the Obama administration. "I could not, after Trump and all the damage he did and the importance I attached to Biden succeeding, not want to contribute if I had the opportunity at the outset. . . . I can run a policy process. The skills translate across policy realms. I just wanted to try to help unscrew what we inherited to the extent I could and try to put real points on the board. That's what I care about."

We hope this book has helped you envision for yourself a rich and rewarding career that makes a real difference in the world. And if nothing else, we hope you can now confidently agree with our view that a career outside academia is far from "second-best." James Graham Wilson reflects on his "brutal" academic job hunt: "Trained academics are not actually part of some priesthood. There is nothing noble about being isolated and unhappy. In few other professions is there the expectation that you ought to move literally anywhere just to have a title. My own mentors are of a generation where they may have been encouraged to go to a place you might not want to be and stick it out for a few years, get the book out, and go elsewhere." In today's glutted academic job market, he says, "that encouragement is about as helpful as betting money on the return of Blockbuster Video."

We also hope this book has made clear to you that there is no single, perfect path to a successful career working in foreign policy (or even on foreign policy)—and, indeed, that embracing serendipity, flexibility, and even failures can help you find a professional role that is true to your passions, values, and personal needs. Kristin Lord is today the president of a nonprofit development organization with an annual budget of nearly $130 million and more than six hundred staff members around the world. She reflects, "Things have worked out really, really well for me. I had a lot of dead ends. I was very poorly equipped for many jobs. I probably almost lost at least two jobs. But I feel like now I have this amazing job. I work with amazing people, I feel like we make a real impact on the world. Some people in my family say you're lucky, you get up every day and you work for an organization that's trying to make the world better. I get up for an organization that's trying to sell people X or Y. . . . So, you know, what do I have to complain about?"

As you try to find your own path, we hope this book helps you navigate through your PhD and beyond as you work on the issues that you care about. Good luck, and keep us posted!

Notes

1. The reference here is to the song in the show *Hamilton*, which you can watch on YouTube: https://www.youtube.com/watch?v=WySzEXKUSZw.

2. James H. Lebovic, review of *Why Intelligence Fails: Lessons from the Iranian Revolution and the Iraq War*, by Robert Jervis, *Perspectives on Politics* 8, no. 4 (2010): 1167–69.

3. Steven A. Holmes, "State Department Balkan Aides Explain Why They Quit," *New York Times*, August 26, 1993, www.nytimes.com/1993/08/26/world/state-dept-balkan-aides-explain-why-they-quit.html.

4. Eliot A. Cohen, "To an Anxious Friend," *American Interest*, 2017, www.the-american-interest.com/2016/11/10/to-an-anxious-friend/.

5. To learn more about Rice's career, read her memoir: Susan Rice, *Tough Love: My Story of the Things Worth Fighting For* (New York: Simon & Schuster, 2019).

Appendix A

Selected Workshops, Summer Programs, and Fellowships

Workshops and Summer Programs

Bridging the Gap, New Era Workshop, https://bridgingthegap project.org
/programs/new-era/

Center for Naval Analyses, Research Student Summer Internship Program,
https://www.cna.org/careers/internship

Clements Center for National Security, Summer Seminar in History and
Statecraft at Beaver Creek, Colorado, https://www.clementscenter.org
/programs/clements-summer-seminar-in-history-and-statecraft

Institute for Defense Analyses, Summer Associate Program, https://www.ida.org
/careers/students-and-recent-graduates/summer-associate-internships-and
-fellowships/summer-associates#

Johns Hopkins School of Advanced International Studies, International Policy
Scholars Consortium and Network (IPSCON), https://sais.jhu.edu/kissinger
/ipscon

RAND Graduate Student Summer Associate Program, https://www.rand.org
/about/edu_op/fellowships/gsap.html

Summer Workshop on the Analysis of Military Operations and Strategy
(SWAMOS), https://www.siwps.org/programs/summer-workshop-on-the
-analysis-of-military-operations-and-strategy/

Fellowships

*Please note that, though all these opportunities support work on policy topics, not all are
based in policy institutions, or even in Washington.*

Advocacy Project, Fellowship, https://www.advocacynet.org/2022-peace
-fellowships/

American Association for the Advancement of Science Fellowship, https://www
.aaas.org/page/fellowship-areas

American Institute for Economic Research (AIER), Graduate Fellowships, https://
www.aier.org/graduate-fellowships/

America in the World Consortium Postdoctoral Fellowships, https://academic
jobsonline.org/ajo/jobs/20304

Asian Development Bank, ADB–Japan Scholarship Program, https://www.adb.org
/work-with-US/careers/japan-scholarship-program/institutions#accordion
-0-8

Association of Women in International Trade Scholarships, https://www.wiit.org
/wii9781647123550ttrU.S.t?page_id=1086

Ax:son Johnson Institute for Statecraft and Diplomacy (AJI), https://sais.jhu.edu
/kissinger/programs/aji

Belfer Center for Science and International Affairs, Research Fellowships, https://
www.belfercenter.org/fellowships

Boren Fellowship, https://www.borenawards.org/

Bright Research Group, Perez Research Fellowship, https://www.brightresearch
group.com/perez-research-fellowship/

Brookings Institution, David M. Rubenstein Fellowship, https://www.brookings
.edu/david-m-rubenstein-fellowship-program/

Bush School, Albritton Center for Grand Strategy, Pre- and Post-Doctoral
Fellowships, https://bUSh.tamu.edu/wp-content/uploads/2020/07/2020
-21CGSFellowshipAdRevised.pdf

Catholic Relief Services, International Development Fellows Program, https://
www.crs.org/about/careers/fellowships

Center for a New American Security Fellow / Associate Fellow, Technology and
National Security Program, https://www.cnas.org/careers/fellow-associate
-fellow-technology-and-national-security-program

Charles Koch Institute, Stand Together Fellowships, https://charleskochinstitute
.org/stand-together-fellowships/koch-associate-program/

Congressional Budget Office, Visiting Scholars, https://www.cbo.gov/about
/careers/visitingscholars

Council of American Overseas Research Centers, Multi-Country Research
Fellowship, https://www.caorc.org/fellowships

Council on Foreign Relations International Affairs Fellowship, https://www.cfr
.org/fellowships/international-affairs-fellowship

Dartmouth College, John Sloan Dickey Center for International Understanding,
Postdoctoral Fellowship Program, https://www.american.edu/sis/centers
/security-technology/opportunities.cfm

Echidna Global Scholars Program, https://www.brookings.edu/echidna-global
-scholars-program/

Elliott School Institute for Security and Conflict Studies, Visiting Scholars
Program, https://iscs.elliott.gwu.edu/visiting-scholars-program/

Fulbright US Student Program, https://us.fulbrightonline.org/about/fulbright
-US-student-program

Grand Strategy, Security, and Statecraft Fellows Program, Harvard–MIT program,
https://ssp.mit.edu/about/fellowships/statecraft-fellows-program

Harvard Law School, Institute for Global Law & Policy, Residential Fellowship
Program, https://iglp.law.harvard.edu/fellows/

Harvard University, Edmond J. Safra Center for Ethics Fellowship-in-Residence,
https://ethics.harvard.edu/pages/fellowships

Hubert H. Humphrey Fellowship Program, https://www.humphreyfellowship.org/

Jefferson Scholars Foundation, National Fellowship, https://www.jefferson
scholars.org/nationalfellowship

John S. McCain Strategic Defense Fellows Program, https://www.whs.mil/mccain
-fellows-program/

John W. Kluge Center Fellowships, https://www.loc.gov/programs/john-w-kluge
-center/chairs-fellowships/fellowships/kluge-fellowships/

Kellogg Institute for International Studies, Visiting Fellowships, https://kellogg
.nd.edu/opportunities/visiting-researchers/about-our-visiting-fellowships
#tab-2014

Notre Dame International Security Center, Hans J. Morgenthau Fellowship,
https://ndisc.nd.edu/people/opportunities/the-notre-dame-international
-security-center-hans-j-morgenthau-fellows/

Notre Dame Postdoctoral Fellowship in Innovative Approaches to Grand Strategy,
https://ndisc.nd.edu/people/opportunities/post-doctoral-fellowship-in
-innovative-approaches-to-grand-strategy/

Postdoctoral Research Scholar in National Security & Intelligence Studies; Arnold
A. Saltzman Institute of War and Peace Studies, Columbia University, https://
www.siwps.org/call-for-applications-postdoctoral-research-scholar-in-national
-security-and-intelligence-studies/

Presidential Management Fellowship (PMF), https://www.pmf.gov/

Public Company Accounting Oversight Board, Fellowship Program, https://
pcaobus.org/careers/econfellowship

Reimagining Democracy Fellowship, Ash Center for Democratic Governance and
Innovation, https://ash.harvard.edu/files/ash/files/reimagining_democracy
_fellowship_job_description_0.pdf?m=1627065048

Rumsfeld Foundation Graduate Fellowship Program, https://www.rumsfeld
foundation.org/public_service/graduate_fellowships

Smith Richardson Foundation, World Politics & Statecraft Fellowship, https://
www.srf.org/programs/international-security-foreign-policy/world-politics
-statecraft-fellowship/

Stanford CISAC (Center for International Security and Cooperation) Fellowships,
https://cisac.fsi.stanford.edu/cisac-fellowships

Stanton Nuclear Security Fellowship, Council on Foreign Relations, https://www
.cfr.org/fellowships/stanton-nuclear-security-fellowship

Stimson Center, South Asia Junior Fellowship, https://www.stimson.org/project
/south-asia-fellowships/

US Institute of Peace, Peace Scholar Competition, https://www.usip.org/grants
-fellowships/fellowships/peace-scholar-fellowship-program

US Institute of Peace, Transatlantic Post-Doc Fellowship for International
Relations and Security (TAPIR) Program, https://www.usip.org/transatlantic
-post-doc-fellowship-international-relations-and-security-tapir-program

Wilson Center Fellowship, https://www.wilsoncenter.org/fellowship-application

Women in Defense, WID Scholar, https://www.womenindefense.net/widscholar
/about-wid-scholar

Appendix B

Selected Washington-Area Institutions Conducting Policy-Relevant Research

For-Profit Institutions

Albright Stonebridge Group, https://www.albrightstonebridge.com/
BAE Systems, https://www.baesystems.com/en/home
Booz Allen Hamilton, https://www.boozallen.com/
CACI International Inc., https://www.caci.com/
DFI International, http://www.dfi-intl.com/
Eurasia Group, https://www.eurasiagroup.net/
McLarty Associates, https://maglobal.com/
Science Applications International Corporation, https://www.saic.com/
Scowcroft Group, https://www.scowcroft.com/

Nonprofit Think Tanks

Africa Center for Strategic Studies, https://africacenter.org/
American Academy of Diplomacy, https://www.academyof diplomacy.org/
American Enterprise Institute, https://www.aei.org/
American Foreign Policy Council, https://www.afpc.org/
Arab American Institute, https://www.aaiusa.org/
Arab Gulf States Institute, https://agsiw.org/
Arms Control Association, https://www.armscontrol.org/
Asia Society Policy Institute, https://asiasociety.org/policy-institute
Aspen Institute, https://www.aspeninstitute.org/
Atlantic Council, https://www.atlanticcouncil.org/
Brookings Institution, https://www.brookings.edu/
Carnegie Endowment for International Peace, https://carnegie endowment.org/
Cato Institute, https://www.cato.org/
Center for Advanced Defense Studies (C4ADS), https://c4ads.org/
Center for American Progress, https://www.americanprogress.org/
Center for a New American Security, https://www.cnas.org/

Center for Climate and Security, https://climateandsecurity.org/
Center for Defense Information Project on Government Oversight (POGO),
    https://www.pogo.org/center-for-defense-information
Center for European Policy Analysis, https://cepa.org/
Center for Global Development, https://www.cgdev.org/
Center for International Policy, https://www.internationalpolicy.org/
Center for Strategic and Budgetary Assessments, https://csbaonline.org/
Center for Strategic and International Studies, https://www.csis.org/
Center for the National Interest, https://cftni.org/
Center for the Study of the Presidency and Congress, https://www.thepresidency.org/
Council on Foreign Relations, https://www.cfr.org/
Council on Hemispheric Affairs, https://www.coha.org/
Economic Policy Institute, https://www.epi.org/
Federation of American Scientists, https://fas.org/
Foreign Policy Research Institute, https://www.fpri.org/
Foundation for Defense of Democracies, https://www.fdd.org/
Foundation for Iranian Studies, https://fis-iran.org/
Fund for Peace, https://fundforpeace.org/
German Marshall Fund of the United States, https://www.gmfus.org/
Henry L. Stimson Center, https://www.stimson.org/
Heritage Foundation, https://www.heritage.org/
Hoover Institution, https://www.hoover.org/
Hudson Institute, https://www.hudson.org/
Institute of Caribbean Studies, https://www.icsdc.org/
Institute for Policy Studies, https://ips-dc.org/
Institute for Science and International Security, https://isis-online.org/
Institute for the Study of War, https://www.understandingwar.org/
Institute for Women's Policy Research, https://iwpr.org/
International Center on Nonviolent Conflict, https://www.nonviolent-conflict.org/
International Institute for Strategic Studies, https://www.iiss.org/
International Strategic Studies Association, https://www.strategicstudies.org/
Jamestown Foundation, https://jamestown.org/
Jewish Institute for National Security of America, https://jinsa.org/
Lexington Institute, https://www.lexingtoninstitute.org/
McCain Institute, https://www.mccaininstitute.org/
Meridian International Center, https://www.meridian.org/
Middle East Institute, https://www.mei.edu/
Middle East Media Research Institute, https://www.memri.org/
Middle East Policy Council, https://mepc.org/
Migration Policy Institute, https://www.migrationpolicy.org/
National Council for US-Arab Relations, https://ncusar.org/
National Research Council, https://tethys.pnnl.gov/organization/national-research
    -council-national-academies-nrc

New America Foundation, https://www.newamerica.org/
Newlines Institute for Strategy and Policy, https://newlinesinstitute.org/about/
Nuclear Threat Initiative, https://www.nti.org/
Peterson Institute for International Economics, https://www.piie.com/
Progressive Policy Institute, https://www.progressivepolicy.org/
Quincy Institute, https://quincyinst.org/
Washington Institute for Business, Government, and Society, https://www.wash
    inst.org/
Washington Institute for Near East Policy, https://www.washingtoninstitute.org/

Federally Funded Research-and-Development Centers

ANSER, https://www.anser.org/
Center for Naval Analyses, https://www.cna.org/
Institute for Defense Analyses, https://www.ida.org/
MITRE Corporation, https://www.mitre.org/
RAND Corporation, https://www.rand.org/

Institutions with Federal Appropriations

Eurasia Foundation, https://www.eurasia.org/
International Republican Institute, https://www.iri.org/
National Endowment for Democracy, https://www.ned.org/
National Democratic Institute, https://www.ndi.org/
US Institute of Peace, https://www.usip.org/
Woodrow Wilson International Center for Scholars, https://www.wilsoncenter.org/

Government "Think Tanks"

Congressional Research Service, https://www.loc.gov/crsinfo/
Defense Advanced Research Projects Agency, https://www.darpa.mil/
Defense Capabilities and Management Team, Government
    Accountability Office, https://www.gao.gov/blog/2014 /03/28/gaos
    -defense-capabilities-and-management-team
Defense Threat Reduction Agency, https://www.dtra.mil/
National Defense University Centers and Institutes, https://www.ndu.edu
    /Research/Centers-and-Institutes/
Policy Planning Staff, Department of State, https://www.state.gov/about-us-policy
    -planning-staff/

Appendix C

Selected Networking Institutions

AFCEA Emerging Professionals in Intelligence Committee (EPIC), https://www.afcea.org/site/?q=intelligence/epic

American Association for Public Opinion Research, https://www.aapor.org/

American Society of Criminology, https://asc41.com/

Association for Applied and Clinical Sociology, https://www.aacsnet.net/

Association of Women in International Trade (WIIT), https://www.wiit.org/wiit about

Black Professionals in International Affairs, https://iabpia.org/what-we-do

Consortium of Practicing & Applied Anthropologists, https://www.copaainfo.org/

Digital Anthropology Group, https://01anthropology.wordpress.com/page/2/

EASA Applied Anthropology Network, https://www.applied-anthropology.com/wwna/

Ethnographic Praxis in Industry Conference, https://www.epicpeople.org/about-epic/

Intelligence and National Security Alliance (INSA) Internship Program, https://www.insaonline.org/about/internships/

International Association of Applied Psychology, https://iaapsy.org/about/

John Quincy Adams Society, https://jqas.org/about-us/

Leadership Council for Women in National Security, https://www.lcwins.org/about

Leading Women of Tomorrow, https://www.leadingwomenoftomorrow.com/

#NatSecGirlSquad, https://www.natsecgirlsquad.com/

Out in National Security, https://www.outinnationalsecurity.org/

Peace, Collaboration, and Development Network, https://pcdn.global/learn/about-us/

Society for Applied Anthropology, https://www.appliedanthro.org/

Sociologists for Women in Society, https://socwomen.org/about/

Truman National Security Project, https://www.trumanproject.org/about/about-us

Washington Association of Professional Anthropologists, https://wapadc.org/about

Washington Network Group, https://washingtonnetworkgroup.com/about/overview/

Women in Defense, https://www.womenindefense.net/about-wid

Women in Government Relations, https://www.wgr.org/page/About_Us

Women in International Security, https://wiisglobal.org/about/
Women of Color Advancing Peace, Security, and Conflict Transformation, https://
    www.wcaps.org/
Women's Foreign Policy Group, https://www.wfpg.org/about-wfpg
Young Professionals in Foreign Policy, https://www.ypfp.org/about/
Young Professionals in International Affairs, https://www.ypiadc.org/overview

Index

AAAS. *See* American Association for
 the Advancement of Science (AAAS)
academia, 2–7, 19, 34–35, 50–52,
 83–84, 89, 110–20
advocacy, 74–75
Agriculture Department, 67
alt-academic careers, 5–6
ambassadorship, 116–18, 130–31
American Association for the Advancement of Science (AAAS), 70, 107
American Dilemma, The (Myrdal), 15
American Enterprise Institute, 16, 106
American Political Science Association, 50, 74
American University, 33
Art, Robert, 35

Barton, Mary, 8, 26, 44, 88–90
Belcher, Emma, 80
Bill & Melinda Gates Foundation,
 79–80
Bonicelli, Paul J., 8, 73, 126–27
Boren Fellowships, 46
Bridging the Gap, 43–44
Brigety, Reuben, 8, 32, 48, 57, 84, 94,
 116–18, 129
Brookings Institution, 5, 27, 76, 103,
 118–20
Brown v. Board of Education, 15

Campbell, Susanna, 8, 27–28, 111
career pathways: academia and,
 110–20; in foreign policy, 101–20;
 mentors and, 110; sponsors and, 110
Carnegie Corporation, 15, 43, 79–80,
 108
casualties, military, 14
Citigroup, 59

Civil Service, 67–68
Clements Center for National Security
 Summer Seminar in History and
 Statecraft, 43–44
Clinton, Bill, 35
Cohen, Eliot, 130
"cold calls," 95
Commerce Department, 64, 67
communication skills, 19–20, 76, 90
community, of knowledge and action,
 122–23
conflict zones, 98–99. *See also* defense
 industry
Congressional Research Service (CRS),
 53, 63, 73–74
Consumer Financial Protection Bu-
 reau, 46–47
contractors, 54, 58, 64, 70–71
Council of the American Geographical
 Society, 51
Council on Foreign Relations, 40, 50,
 59, 69–70, 74, 117
CRS. *See* Congressional Research
 Service (CRS)

Daalder, Ivo, 9, 25–26, 118
Danon, Zoe, 9, 72, 74
Davidson, Janine, 104
decision-making, 14, 18–19
Defense Department, 39, 45, 65, 69,
 102–3
defense industry, 103–5. *See also* conflict zones
Del Rosso, Stephen, 9, 15, 28, 80, 105
deterrence, 15
diplomacy, coercive, 15, 117
disciplinary approaches, 13–14
doctoral program. *See* PhD

Doshi, Rush, 39
Drezner, Daniel, 24
Durbin, Erik, 9, 45–46, 102, 110–11, 114, 125

Eurasia Group, 59, 78–79
Evans, Alexandra, 31, 43, 83–84, 89
excepted service, 66, 69
Executive Branch, 64–72
expertise, 26, 46, 63, 67, 69–71, 92, 94–96

Farmer, Paul, 113
federally funded research and development centers (FFRDCs), 77
Federal Reserve Board, 58
FFRDCs. See federally funded research and development centers (FFRDCs)
flexibility, 34, 67, 96–98
Flournoy, Michèle, 22
Foreign Commercial Service, 64
foreign policy: career pathways in, 101–20; decision makers in, 63–64; ecosystem, 62–81; Executive Branch in, 64–72; job seeking in, 83–100; Legislative Branch in, 72–74; making a difference working in, 121–32; non-profits in, 74–75; private sector in, 77–79; think tanks in, 76–77; working in vs. working on, 12–23. See also policy work
Foreign Service, 55, 64, 66–69, 95, 130
foundations, 79–80
Friend, Alice Hunt, 9, 26–30, 40, 93–94
Future Strategy Forum, 86, 94

Gaddis, John Lewis, 119
Galpern, Steve, 9, 89–90, 93, 97, 99, 123
Gates Foundation, 79–80
George, Alexander, 15
goals, questions and, 13–22
graduate school, opportunities in, 24–49. See also PhD
Gregorian, Vartan, 80

Hicks, Kathleen, 39, 86

intelligence community, 71–72, 114–15
International Affairs Fellowship, 50, 74, 114, 117
International Criminal Investigative Training Assistance Program, 65
International Monetary Fund, 58–59, 62
International Policy Scholars Consortium and Network (IPSCON), 43
internships, 44–47, 84
interpersonal skills, 21, 92–95
Interpol, 65
IPSCON. See International Policy Scholars Consortium and Network (IPSCON)

Jacobs, Matthew, 9, 84, 86, 91, 114–15
jargon, 19–20
Jenkins, Bonnie, 39
Jervis, Robert, 127
job seeking: communication in, 90–92; flexibility in, 96–97; in foreign policy, 83–100; interpersonal skills in, 92–95; mind-set in, 88–90; networking skills in, 92–95; skill set presentation in, 84–88; work/life balance and, 97–100; writing in, 90–92. See also career pathways
John S. McCain Strategic Defense Fellows Program, 69
journalism, 30–31
journals, 80
Justice Department, 65

Kahn, Robert, 9, 35, 58–59, 78
Kaplan, Morgan, 24, 28–29, 36, 38, 78, 81, 86–89
Kaufman, Bill, 33
Kelleher, Catherine, 48, 106
Kelman, Herbert, 33, 113
Kilcullen, David, 104
knowledge, community of, 122–23
Kopp, Harry, 67
Krugman, Paul, 35

Labor Department, 64
leadership, 60, 95, 116–18, 130–31
Leadership Council for Women in National Security, 42

Legislative Branch, 72–74
Lord, Kristin, 9, 25, 92, 114
Lustick, Ian, 105

Madan, Tanvi, 9, 19, 27, 33, 35, 76, 83, 87, 118–20, 122
Massachusetts Institute of Technology (MIT) Security Studies Program (SSP), 34
McAlister, Melani, 49n2
McArdle, Jennifer, 9, 37, 40, 78–79, 85, 95, 110, 124
McChrystal, Stanley, 104
McLachlan, Paul, 9, 40, 78–79, 88, 95
membership organization, 41–42
mentors, 35, 42, 48, 51, 69, 99–100, 105–7, 110, 124–25
Mercy Corps, 36–37, 54, 98, 113–14
mind-set, 88–90
mission, 59–60
Moore Capital Management, 59
moral compass, 127–32
Myrdal, Gunnar, 15

Naland, John, 67
National Intelligence Council, 58
NATO. See North Atlantic Treaty Organization (NATO)
networking skills, 41, 92–95
New Era workshop, 40–41
nonprofits, 6, 63–64, 74–75, 112–14
North Atlantic Treaty Organization (NATO), 19

Obama, Barack, 22, 35
Office of International Affairs (Labor Department), 64
Office of International Affairs (Treasury Department), 64
Office of Terrorism and Financial Intelligence (Treasury Department), 64
opportunities, in graduate school, 24–49

Personal Service Contractors (PSCs), 70–71
PhD: advantages of, in policy work, 29–32; direction and, 26; expertise and, 26; isolation in, 21; journalism and, 30–31; need for, 25–29; program, what to look for, 32–35; for self, 27–28; in social science, 4, 6
Plana, Sara, 9, 30, 43, 45, 48, 85–86, 99, 102, 112
PMF. See Presidential Management Fellowship (PMF)
policy analysis: constraints in, 16–18; doctoral degree and, 13; from, to action, 22–23; PhD in, 29–32; time frame in, 16–17
policy communication, 20
policy work: academia and, 6–7; constraints in, 17; envisioning oneself in, 50–60; legacy with, 5; PhD in, advantages of, 29–32; in practice, 22–23; skill set in, 12, 20; solo work in, 56–59; in team, 56–59; thinker-doer continuum in, 52–54; time constraints in, 17; turning toward, 102–10. See also career pathways; foreign policy
policy workplace, as context, 18–22
Posen, Barry, 9, 34–35
positivism, 59–60, 125–27
Powell, Colin, 116, 128
Presidential Management Fellowship (PMF), 68
private sector, 18, 55, 62, 77–79, 95, 110
PSCs. See Personal Service Contractors (PSCs)
puzzle solving, 59–60

questions: analytical, 22–23; goals and, 13–22

Rand, Dafna, 9, 15–16, 36–37, 39, 45–46, 54, 57–58, 89, 98
RAND Corporation, 77, 104
Rathjens, George, 33
Ratner, Ely, 39
Recent Graduates Program, 69
Reisser, Wesley, 1, 5, 9, 24, 28, 32, 50–51, 65, 88, 90, 96, 99, 108–10, 112
research methods, 35–38
Research on International Policy Implementation Lab (RIPIL), 27–28
research skills, 35, 76, 85–86

resources, as constraint, 17
Revkin, Mara, 1–2, 9, 36–37, 39, 85–86, 91, 98, 103
Rice, Condoleezza, 48, 107–8, 131
Rice, Susan, 10, 27, 130–31
RIPIL. *See* Research on International Policy Implementation Lab (RIPIL)
risk evaluation, 14
Robbins, Carla Anne, 10, 30, 48, 51, 102, 111
Rosenwasser, Jon, 10, 37–38, 40, 49, 112, 123
Ruger, William, 35, 80, 110, 114
Ruina, Jack, 33

Savranskaya, Svetlana, 40
Schake, Kori, 10, 16, 25–26, 48, 90–92, 99, 106–7
Schelling, Thomas, 48, 106
Scott, Rick, 73
shorthand, 19–20
Silicon Valley, 88
Simpson, Erin, 10, 59–60, 78, 96, 103–5, 112, 122
skills: communication, 19–20, 76, 90; interpersonal, 21, 92–95; networking, 92–95; presentation of, 84–88; research, 35–38, 76, 85–86
Sloat, Amanda, 39
social change, 1, 125
social science: applied *vs.* theoretical, 12, 15; defense industry and, 103–5; knowledge building in, 18; PhD programs in, 4; PhD recipients in, 6; teams and, 56

solo work, 56–59
sponsors, 110
Stam, Al, 104
State Department, 18, 64–68, 108–9, 112
Steinberg, James, 35, 119
summer programs, 44–47

teaching, 50–52. *See also* academia
teams, 56–59, 88–89, 124–25
Tecott, Rachel, 86
thinker-doer continuum, 52–54
think tanks, 63–64, 76–77, 118–20
time frame, in policy analysis, 16–17
Treasury Department, 64
tribe, 40–47

University of Texas at Austin, 33
university presses, 80–81
US Agency for International Development (USAID), 37, 39, 46, 54, 57, 64–65, 67
USAJOBS, 68

vision, 59–60

Wallander, Celeste, 39
Western, Jon, 129
Wilson, James Graham, 10, 40, 91
Wolfe, Rebecca, 10, 33, 51, 112–14
work/life balance, 97–100
workshops, 42–44
World Bank, 59, 62, 104
writing, 90–92

About the Authors

James Goldgeier is a professor of international relations at American University's School of International Service, where he served as dean from 2011 to 2017. He holds visiting appointments at Stanford University and the Brookings Institution, and he is a senior adviser to Bridging the Gap, which promotes policy-relevant academic research. He has served on the National Security Council staff and currently serves as chair of the State Department's Historical Advisory Committee and as a member of the Secretary of State's International Security Advisory Board. He received his doctorate in political science from the University of California, Berkeley.

Tamara Cofman Wittes has held senior roles in government, the nonprofit sector, and think tanks. She served as a deputy assistant secretary of state in the Obama administration and as a senior sanctions policy adviser in the Biden administration. She spent sixteen years as a foreign policy scholar at the Brookings Institution, where she directed the Center for Middle East Policy from 2012 to 2017. She is a founder of the Leadership Council for Women in National Security and is an adjunct professor in Georgetown University's School of Foreign Service. She received a doctorate in government from Georgetown.